Gaze of Thunder
—A reverse anthropological poetics
Followed by "Poetry as Resistance"
Author: Eddy Toussaint Tontongi

Trilingual Press:
PO Box 391206, Cambridge, MA 02139/ Tel. 617-331-2269
Email: trilingualpress@tanbou.com

Graphic design: David Henry, www.davidphenry.com

Edited by Jill Netchinsky, PhD, Trilingual Press' English Editor

The cover photo is an adaptation from Anna Wexler's
Vodou Flag for Magazine *Tanbou* (1997)

ISBN 978-1-936431-46-5
ISBN 10: 1-936431-46-7

Library of Congress Control Number: 2024952455

Printed in the United States of America, first
published edition: October 2025

Trilingual Press, Cambridge, Massachusetts

Gaze of Thunder

—**An anthropopoetic journey**
(Poems)

followed by Poetry as Resistance
(Essay)

TONTONGI

Trilingual Press, Cambridge, Massachusetts

Books published by the author

Tyaka Poetica (poems and essays in Haitian and French, ed. Trilingual Press, Boston, Massachusetts, 2023).

La Parole indomptée / Memwa Baboukèt (essays in French and Haitian, L'Harmattan, Paris, France, 2015).

Sèl pou dezonbifye Bouki (essays in Haitian– ed. Trilingual Press, Boston, Massachusetts, 2013).

In the Beast's Alley (poems in English, ed. Trilingual Press, Boston, Massachusetts, 2012).

Poetica Agwe, poems and essays in Haitian, French, and English (Trilingual Press, Boston, Massachusetts, 2011).

Critique de la francophonie haïtienne (essais en français et en haïtien, éd. l'Harmattan, Paris, France, 2007).

The Vodou Gods' Joy/Rejwisans lwa yo (epic, bilingual poems English-Ayisyen, ed. Tambour, Boston, Massachusetts, 1997).

The Dream of Being (poems in English co-authored with Gary Hicks; ed. New Strategy Book, Boston, Massachusetts, 1991).

La présidence d'Aristide : Entre le défi et l'espoir (français et ayisyen, éd. New Strategy Books, Boston, Massachusetts, 1990).

Cri de rêve (poems in French and Haitian, éd. New Strategy Book, Boston, Massachusetts, 1986).

Books edited or co-edited by the author

This Land, My Beloved: A Trilingual Anthology of Contemporary Haitian Poetry. Edited by Elizabeth Brunazzi, Denizé Lauture & Tontongi, ed. Trilingual Press, 2023.

The Anthology of Liberation Poetry, English poems co-edited with Jill Netchinsky (TP, Boston, Massachusetts, 2012).

Voices of the Sun: The Anthology of Haitian Writers Published in the Review Tanbou / Vwa Solèy pale : Antoloji ekriven ayisyen ki pibliye nan revi Tanbou / Les Voix du Soleil : Anthologie des écrivains haïtiens publiés dans la revue Tanbou (TP, Boston, Massachusetts, 2009).

Poets Against the Killing Fields, poems in English (TP, Boston, Massachusetts, 2007).

Table of Contents

    Books published by the author 6
Introduction 11
    Poetry as paradigmatic inquiry 11
    Codifying memories in unsettling times 12
    Hope again for Haiti. 17
    The Other as Me and Us 18
    Finally, on my embrace of English 22
First Period Poetics 25
    A Word of Wisdom to the Disappointed Voters. 27
    Thought on a Blue and Red Weekend 28
    Climbing up Lady Liberty on a Fourth of July. 29
    I Heard the Voice of the Wife 30
    If You Think... 33
    Annex to "If You Think..." 37
    Remembering the Blizzards of 2015 in Boston. 38
    The Causalities of Evil. 41
    Part I: The Masters of Quake Land 41
    Part II: The Intersection of Suffering and Resistance 44
    The Business of Saving Lives 49
    The Children at Aganman's Gate. 51
    The Dead Boy on the Beach 54
    The Emperor's Last Speech. 56
    The Long March From Charlottesville to Boston. 60
    The Panhandler. 64
    On Giving 66
    Terrorism of the Mind 67
    The Thousand Sins of Piety and Love. 71
    The Tragic Waltz of the Wicked Eagles. 74
    It's New York. 83
    What Resilience Ain't 86
    Why Did Dunkin' Donut Empty the Place of Undesirable
    People?. 88
    Glory on 17th October. 90
    Where the Square Wanderer Sleeps 92
    Haiti Is Not What You Say, Mr. Tèt-Mato. 94
Second Period Poetics 99
    Mawonnaj (Marooning) 100
    March 31st, 2017. 101

April 1st, 2011 102
April 1st, 2017 (continued). 103
How Do You Tell the End?. 104
Orwellian Three-Month Time. 105
Collective Scream of Joy. 106
A Drink From a Beautiful Stranger 107
A Drink From a Beautiful Stranger (continued) 108
Deconstructing Our Mental State 109
Bad News 110
Get Rid of Your Hang Up. 111
It's Not the Race, Nor the Color, Idiot 112
Which One of the Oligarchs? 113
As Devoted a Woman Could Be 114
No Reversing Role 115
Daring Little Bug. 116
What About If We Talked? 117
P.S.. 118
"Killing Me Softly With His Song" 119
If He Stays He's Staying For Life. 120
Never Provoke a Madman 121
Destiny and Living. 123
The Bar as Oasis. 124
Thanks God That the Dance of Death Was Canceled 125
How Do You Change a Bad Narrative? 126
A Strange Time For a Strange Country. 128
What Does Really Count?. 129
Revelation 130
He Is as Apple Pie as US-America. 131

Third Period Poetics. 133

Carefree Geese on the Charles River. 134
The Lifeline Power of a Smile. 135
For the Traumatized and the Departed 136
Goodbye, Aunt Lili 137

Fourth Period Poetics. 139

Where Do We Start Counting? 140
Laurels for the Dead 142
How Could Your Eyes Stay Dry? 145
Columbia U Saves the Soul 147
Boston's Vigilant Watchful Eyes 149
Lamentations For Two Police Killings. 150

    Part I. Sayed Faisal................................... 150
    Part II. Tyre Nichols.................................. 152
    Post-Scriptum 153
    Mariupol 155
    Moments in US Presidential History 156
    Haiti Is Her Name.................................... 164
    What Might Have Been............................... 167
    Moments in Neo-Nero's Return....................... 170

Epilogue in Three Parts................................ 175
    I. Fascism's Specter, Alienation and Self-Mutilation....... 177
    II. On Anticipatory Obedience 177
    II. Poetry as Resistance 181

From the left: **Tontongi with Georges Anglade** in the house of Haitian educator Berhmann Narcisse in Mattapan (Boston, MA) in 1984.

Introduction

The following poems are together testimonials to my living at a certain time and in a certain place in the United States of America, snatch-short memories of fugitive instants, and long-term aspirations and dreams for a better world. The book consists of four parts, the first containing poems that codify memories of the Trump candidacy and administration from the years 2016 to 2021 (each instant feeling like an eternity). Those poems also encompass the heroic and persevering resistance the people mounted to counter the nightmare.

The second part lays out a series of short, conceptual poems and texts, impregnated with philosophical insights and lyrical reasoning that mix prosaic form and poetic symphony. This part captures what I call the *fugitive moments*, those that come *à l'improviste*, unexpectedly, in the contingency of everyday living, in the slow passing of time. The poems in the first part, as well in the second, can deservedly be construed in phenomenological fashion as a kind of anthropological poetics or *anthropopoetics*, evidentiary revelation of my being-there in the United States in that particular moment. Being there at the moment when History is being written, being there as part of a complex world within the USA. Being there in this particular juncture and conjuncture provides me with a huge source of material and intellectual sustenance, despite the many obvious stressors and apprehensions it entails.

The third part includes poems conceived and composed during the Covid-19 pandemic, giving a window into my *affect* of the time. How could a poet live those dreadful and macabre moments and not put down something on paper? The same is true for the fourth (and last) part of the book: How could I live the genocidal horrors in the Israeli-Palestinian conflict and not put down something on paper?

Poetry as paradigmatic inquiry

Having lived most of my adult life in exile in Northern countries, my essays and poems are both anthropological data and lyrical testimonials. Only this time the anthropology is reversed; instead of the colonizer looking at the colonized as object, it is the colonized who is now looking at the colonizer—or the inheritor of the colonizer—, perhaps not as object but as anthropological interest. For once the North is being scrutinized by a gaze that is, as Frantz Fanon would say, "a conscience of itself," and not a reflection of its own megalomania.

The notion of a *reverse anthropology* breaks new ground in that, for a rare time in recent intellectual history, perhaps since the *Négritude* movement and the Fanonian affirmation of the Other as subject, the Western paradigm of valorization is challenged by an "Outsider" gaze who questions everything, including not only the unjust nature of the ambient power relations, but also the intellectual justification they propose. Indeed, this re-affirmation of the self is essentially an intellectual and paradigmatic inquiry that returns, reverses, displaces, the one-sided gaze of Eurocentrism and its frame of reference, from North-South to South-North, by what Fanon called the "gaze of the Other," questioning its normality-producing cultural outlook posed as universal prototype. The observer is now being observed, the seer seen[1]

My living under Trump in the United States can only compare to living under Papa Doc and Baby Doc Duvalier in Haiti as far as the amount of actual and anticipated catastrophes is concerned. Many of the poems can attest to that. All four parts of the collection are interrelated in that they represent important moments of my life here; they show that my poetic temerity can be pushed to a point where philosophical insight and poetic impulse are intermingled in a state of elemental unity of *complétude*. I've vowed to struggle against the horrors deliberately inflicted on others for dubious, selfish reasons, and to use the riches of experience that I have accumulated to find meaning in the simplest moments and feelings.

Codifying memories in unsettling times

Analyzing the reality of US political life during the decade covered by this book (2015–2025), an acute observer would define it as troublesome and concerning. Since perhaps the U.S. Civil War and the Post-Reconstruction eras—notwithstanding the right-wing, over the top candidacies of George Wallace and Patrick Buchanan—, never had a candidacy and a presidency come so close to destroying the U.S. system of government. Until now, the pretense of governing to uphold the rule of law was universally respected, even though some have tried to corrupt it. However, today the perversion of the public sphere is happening in the open, in plain view. Only in the United States—as the proverbial exceptionalism goes—can a president who tempers with witnesses and jury, openly obstructs justice, gives pardon to harvest political gain, lies repeatedly in his official functions, insults people through his social media proclamations on a daily basis, uses his access to enrich himself and his family, remain president for so long? Nero stayed for thirteen years one would say, but, see what he had done to Rome…

Many of the poems included here were written in a moment when the political institutions of the United States were under unrelenting assault from the Trump administration and its supporters in the Congress. Besides Trump's insults to Haiti and the whole continent of Africa, calling them "shithole countries," there was the open subornation of the House of Representative Intelligence Committee, a body with an oversight duty over the Executive, by its chairman, Devin Nunes, who attempted to manufacture a pretext to force Deputy Attorney General Rod Rosenstein to disclose classified information related to the investigation of Trump's collusion with the Russian government during the 2016 presidential elections.

The years 2017–2021 in particular could very well have the distinction of being among the most nefarious in the US history, even on a list that includes the genocide of the indigenous inhabitants, the horrific slavery regime, and the Post-Reconstruction period. This time the evil-doing is done not by the back door or in the dark of night, but in the spotlight of governmental edicts and media reporting. The Trump administration's Muslim ban, its legitimation of the Neo-Nazi's Charlottesville hateful march, Trump's racial animus toward Black athletes, his disdain toward non-European countries, the arbitrary detention and deportation of migrants and refugees, and the caging of their children like animals, the gutting of the Environmental Protection Agency's ecological regulations and safeguards, the withdrawal from the Paris Climate Agreement, the sanctioning and tacit applauding of racist cops killing Black men and women as if their lives didn't matter, the incitation to racial hatred among the US populations by emphasizing what separates them rather than what unites them; the oddly illogical, unilateral withdrawal from the Iran Nuclear Deal, the mangling of truth and its opposite—lie—as if they were interchangeable, the sowing of purposeful confusion between fact and non-fact, the manipulation of people's genuine frustration with the system due to their exploitation and exclusion from mainstream social advancement, the continual demonization of recent immigrants (everyone else being *also* immigrant although of a less recent vintage); the debasement of the country's image in the world and its degrading influence to the point of being the laughing punch line of world politics; the abandonment of the Kurds, the shake-down of the Ukraine president, the demand that he provide dirt on Trump's domestic political rivals in exchange for economic and military assistance; all of that constituted a tragedy: that of a proud, historically successful country diminished to a lamentable status of mere defender of anything-goes Trump because of personal gain or imperatives of profit for capitalism

As both a consciousness coming from the other side of the Western hemisphere living in otherness, and the embodiment, as a poet, of universal value of human transcendence and elevation, I want my poetry to be not a mere anti-Trump poetics, but rather a poetics that honors the humanist finality of our political engagement. A Polish immigrant poet once told me his demons in the Trump era had been a daily consumption of horrors and continual anticipation of darkness, even in the brightest ray of light. How could poetry exist in the Trump era? To pose the question that way becomes equivalent to saying: How could poetry have existed and survived in the Hitler era? Yes, unlike Theodor Adorno's original assertion (later reconsidered) that "to write poetry after Auschwitz is barbaric," poetry is in itself a potent element and means for wisdom and resistance.

How could poetry have existed in Papa Doc's era? Naturally, poetry continued to exist in both cases, for it never ceased to exist. Even in the many Nazi concentration camps spread around Eastern Europe. How can poetry exist in Hell? Poetry had existed even at Fort-Dimanche, the infamous torture-prison of the Duvaliers.

How did immigrants born in another country—naturalized or not, documented or not—live in the United States in the era of Trump? How did they endure the ambient atmosphere of hatred of the Other displayed in official pronouncements by the government and in the media? How did they live their humanity and "otherness" in a societal environment of hostile sentiments toward them? These were the questions I asked myself as to what degree Trump's rhetoric and actual decisions of his administration shaped and affected the existential well-being of the immigrants and refugees. I witnessed that insidious impact of atmospheric negativities in my capacity as a community worker in the Greater Boston area. I've known people with duly legal status who were desperately worried that I.C.E.[2] would take it away. There were others who needed food but refused to apply for federal nutrition assistance programs because of fear of deportation. Under the guise of Trump's litany of antics, first Attorney General Jeff Sessions, then AG William Barr worked tirelessly, in silence, to undermine the foundations of the modern democratic state that United States has strived to be.

The state of things in this country under Trump was lived by many as a daily, if not hourly, nightmare amplified by the news media playing along with Trump in making it an entertaining circus. It saddened my heart to see a country which was for a time an object of attraction for much of suffering humanity become a repellent object of ridicule for the world. I knew well that the history of this country is a long alternation between longing toward the wonders of human magnanimity, and regression to the lowest instincts of malfeasance and exclusion, but living it at the time in daily life was a more painful experience.

Fortunately, the United States, as dynamic a country as any, is not reductive to Trump. It is also the country of jazz music and of the great upheavals leading to the workers' May Day and the 40-hour work week. The struggle for workers' rights was at one point in the 19th century so advanced in this country that Marx and Engels had hoped that the first Socialist revolution would take place here.

Equally fortunate is the fact the United States is also the country of Therese Patricia Okoumou, a young black woman from Ghana, who climbed up the Statue of Liberty in New York City on the 4th of July 2018, the independence day of the US nation, having gained her courage, as I said in the poem dedicated to her, from the millions of people who, the preceding Saturday, took to the streets in most of the big cities in the United States to protest, horrified as they were by the images of children being separated from their parents at the Mexico-United States border, and "*put into cages while their parents were taken to jails.*" Therese P. Okounou wanted on this solemn day, and in the name of a more noble and higher ideal, that *"Lady Liberty be her witness in exposing governmental atrocities."*[3]

There is also the United States of Ann M. Donnelly, the obscure judge of a federal district in Brooklyn, New York, who blocked nationwide, at the request of the American Civil Liberties Union (ACLU), the Trump-ordered banishment of people from seven Muslim countries, citing the "irreparable damage" that it had caused. There is the United States of Bob Ferguson, the Attorney General of the state of Washington, who used the powers of his office to block and challenge, through the courts, many of the Trump administration's ill-conceived executive orders, including the Muslim ban, the mistreatment of migrants and their families.

There were many other lawyers and activists for human dignity and human rights who descended upon the southern border and northern airports to intercede on behalf of the migrants, refugees, and returning immigrants. It is this United States, that other side of the country, that worked in unison with efforts to relieve human suffering in the name of a humanistic ideal; yes, it is this country which I made my refuge outside of Haiti, and which I was so glad the voters of the elections of 2020 saved from the Trumpian shipwreck.

Naturally, as we now know, it was for a short duration, since this same Donald Trump would return to power in 2025! I say in a another text, the United States is far from being angelic: "[It is] the country that invented jazz, rap and the Internet, and also who led an exterminating war against the indigenous Indians and against Vietnam; the country whose scientists are exploring interstellar spaces, and which at the same time believes in the simplest, unscientific ideas; the country that helps almost all the peoples of the earth, and also which destroyed Haitian agriculture and imposed Michel Martelly as president; the country that elected President Barack Obama, and also Donald Trump."[4]

During Trump's first term, although there were enough reasons to despair, I refused to follow that path. Having once compared Trump to Nero, I wished like the latter the Trump presidency would soon be irrelevant, and would in the future evoke what we should strive *not* to be or become, serving as a vibrant reminder of how imperative is the struggle for a better life, for a better humanity, for working to achieve a better state of being, living, and feeling.

I remain convinced—both as a poet dreaming of the Multiverse of splendors and as a critic of the historical process—, that with the awareness of what it loses if it does nothing, the country will straighten itself and correct the Trump deviational overgrowth in due course. It is its democratic future that is at stake.[5]

This future, as it now stands after the reelection of Trump, is quite challenging to those who believe in the democratic rule of law. The neo-fascist project, with totalitarian overtones and manipulated religious fervor, known as Project 2025, is pressing for a complete overhaul of the US sociopolitical system. It has the merit of being clear and not shy about its unconstitutional program.

Spearheaded by the Heritage Foundation and largely supported by the American conservative movement under the guidance of the influential Federalist Society, a legal organization that advocates a textual and originalist interpretation of the United States Constitution, the program of Project 2025 seeks to return the United States to the era of white supremacy that preceded the civil rights movement. Many recent Supreme Court decisions, including the 2022 Dobbs decision that invalidated Roe v. Wade, the more than fifty-year-old legal precedent that protected women's right to abortion and choice in matters concerning their health care, or the ones that ended Affirmative Action and weakened civil rights laws, are part of Project 2025's agenda.

The prospect of Project 2025 being implemented (whether now or in the future) is all the more frightening, given that it is inspired by a man, Donald Trump, who has called his political opponents "vermin" to be eradicated and accused immigrants of "stealing jobs" from Blacks and Latinos, as if they were confined, as in the days of slavery, to a certain type of labor. Project 2025 says outright that it wants to "deconstruct" the apparatus of the administrative state, as Steve Bannon, Trump's principal ideological inspiration and strategist, has advocated, in short, to "institutionalize Trumpism." "It is not enough for conservatives to win elections, "the Project 2025 website states. "If we are going to rescue the country from the grip of the radical Left, we need both a governing agenda and the right people in place, ready to carry this agenda out on day one of the next conservative administration."

In terms of political theater (and strategy), this Republican project and the prospect of a second Trump presidency caused such alarm that it forced Democrats to redouble their efforts to replace the candidacy of the incumbent president, Joseph Biden, considered too old at 81, with his vice-president, Kamala Harris, to lead the fight against the Trumpist specter. This electoral tactic profoundly changed the game. It proved that the intrinsic power of the biopolitical dynamism can perform miracles when used boldly and creatively. The energy generated was such at some point that it seemed not to matter, three months before the election, whether Donald Trump wins or loses, because the forces that were generated to fight and resist this draconian program were made aware, mobilized, and ready to take them on. Naturally, the question was always in my mind, even unexpressed then: Would the upgrade to a Kamala Harris and Tim Walz administration be enough to ward off and curb the fascist specter that hangs over the country?

Hope again for Haiti

Haiti's crisis of 2018–2024 has three overlapping dimensions that render any short-term solution immediately obsolete. Why? Because the root causes are ignored by the predominant power-brokers, both foreign and local, that are spearheading the crisis resolution process and which see any initiative that addresses its causality as contrary to their interests.

The three dimensions are: 1) the weight of historical background on the behavior of current actors; 2) the process of putrefaction and degradation of a political system in its failing stage; and 3) the interplay of the imperialist reflexes of foreign powers with both the reactionary politics of their allies from the traditional Haitian ruling elite, and the myopic views and interests of opportunist politicians from the lower middle classes—each of whom feels threatened by the popular protests demanding fundamental change.

At this writing (December 2024), eight months after the installation of the Transitional Presidential Council, and six months after the arrival of the first contingent of the Kenya-led multinational police force, the question remains the same (although moot in a certain way): How to honor the principled position against foreign intervention when bands of criminals armed with heavy automatic weapons maraud through much of capital Port-au-Prince and other parts of the country, sowing terror, death and mayhem, often targeting the less fortunate citizens? Do you send cavalries of mercenaries—totally indifferent to the cause of justice and democracy—to quash them and impose the will of their patrons, or seek alternative, less bloody ways to bring about the desired fundamental change?

The critical Haitian case demonstrates, once again, where imperialist desires for control by countries such as the United States, France, England and Canada in particular, end up when there is no counterforce to restrain them. The resistant forces of Haiti should continue to insist that Haiti is a sovereign nation, with its own interests. Whether or not there are foreign powers who may genuinely take to heart Haitian problematics, Haitians should not expect another nation, however sympathetic its president, king or prime minister, to come to "save" them. The quip attributed to Charles de Gaulle is well taken in this instance: "States have no friends, they only have interests," especially the great powers.

Eventually, the imperialist powers must let Haiti live the course of its history, help it when necessary, but above all let it live its historical journey, its destiny. Imperialism, like paternalism, obstructs the natural development of nations. Empire must come to this conclusion. How to avoid the dictatorship of armed gangs that aspire to state power is perhaps one of the occasions when the country really needs help from its true friends—without trading it for its fundamental right to self-determination.

Just as in the United States, Haiti's chaos and violence benefit a particular political milieu. Petty interests, capitalist greed and fascism generally thrive in such atmosphere, as we may see clearly in the past as in the present.

The example of the Obama administration's behavior in Haiti following the devastating earthquake of 2010 is very revealing in this sense, for Haiti did not need paternalistic charity from a benevolent Big Brother, but rather respect for its right to self-determination and to a development choice that would be specifically its own.

In the midwifing of a new Haiti, to use the term of *New York Times* columnist Lydia Polgreen, what Haiti really needs today is not imperialist interference in its affairs (however "humanitarian" one may want to portray it), but rather gestures of solidarity for Haiti's enormous historical contribution to the liberation struggle of the other peoples—including the embryonic United States, Latin America, and even Greece.

Above all, France must return (through negotiation or per its own initiative) the equivalent of the 21 billion dollars in gold francs that it took from Haiti via the indemnity imposed on it in 1825 for its independence and whose balance of payment was passed to City Bank of New York following the 1915–1934 US occupation of Haiti, a historic scam which cost the young nation its entire development project.

The security imperative is certainly important for a people who suffer so much from the arbitrariness of bands of armed, bloodthirsty bandits but any security strategy, to be viable, must be an all-encompassing approach, taking place within the framework of a serious national discussion to validate the requirements of the Constitution. Any other approach would be just an artifice forged by foreign powers to deceive and strengthen their local puppets and servants to the detriment of a truer nation-building perspective, as History has unfortunately shown too many times.

With its great, vibrant, and rich culture, a national language spoken throughout the territory, an ever-resilient people, reportedly immense mining resources, a formidable diaspora living throughout the world, a generous history of solidarity with other oppressed peoples, Haiti has a great chance to recover, because Haiti, as I have long avowed, is the project of Being, one of the founding countries of our modernity. It requires new, revolutionary politics and strategy to honor the grand vision of its original project.[6]

The Other as Me and Us

As the philosopher François Julien has so well articulated, thinking about alterity is already thinking similarity with the Other; even in the most oppositional situations, he says, there is the possibility of conjunction: "To think is to penetrate, by crossing the oppositions forged by language, how opposites, being thus linked to each other, thereby discover themselves dependent on each other."[7]

I consider the predisposition to accentuate empathetic communality with the Other as a victory over the racist and xenophobic conceptuality which presents the "Other" as enemy or as having a priori hostile intentions towards "Us". In short, it is a push towards the impasse of a false duality or dichotomy between Us and Them, between Me and the Other, between those judging themselves to be "natural belongers" against the undesirables contaminating their living space—the immigrants. This last term—living space—obviously refers to the Nazis' objective of getting rid of any human group that they consider capable of "infecting" their living environment.

There is a relocation of human beings' habitat, of their right to a space—at least their right to a thoughtful, non-imperialist, non-destructive use of the geographical space of living—which profoundly handicaps the person who is prevented from exercising it and whose absence constitutes a significant deficiency in their quality of life, or even in their existential completeness. If you doubt that, just ask any unhoused person.

This gaze of the Other, me, toward the Big Brother from the North and on the West in general, is also full of introspection and self-criticism on the refocusing of the gaze. Have I become the center? Or should there be a center and a periphery? Or again, can a center exist without the great means of power to dominate and dictate?

Our *altérisation* of the people from the imaginary South is imposed from the outside. When Donald Trump called Haiti and the entire African continent "shitholes," I felt wounded both in myself and my civic validity. If it was only an utterance, why did I allow myself to be burdened by such insignificance? Still, I made it my duty to defend the honor of Haiti, and also of Africa, and of all the immigrant workers humiliated by Trump. I wrote a poem, the only weapon I had, about this insult, where I denounced him as a son of the rich parents who had been coddled for too long, a *"white supremacist in the White House... [driven by] the power of greed..."*[8]

Trump's 2024 election promises to the US-American population are terrifying enough in themselves: elect himself dictator for a day, mass deportation of undocumented migrants; to purge the career administrative workforce of anti-Trumpians, "retribution" against political enemies, dismantlement of the federal administration, etc. In short, it seemed to be the agenda of a man who did not want to be elected, or, if that happened, to have given himself the power to abolish the entire constitutional democratic order.

In Donald Trump's defense—and this is perhaps one of the rare compliments I have ever paid him—the animal that is cornered always defends itself and there's nothing more worrying for a human being than the specter of the loss of freedom. Appreciating the enormity of his crimes—political, civil and criminal—and the personal hardship and public affront that their punishment would cause him, it is clear that for Trump, this is a question of his personal freedom, if not of life and death. Like Benjamin Netanyahu in Israel to whom the genocidal war against the Palestinians in Gaza and the West Bank provides a sort of insurance against his indictment for crimes of another nature, Trump hoped that his overreach against the rule of law would destabilize the functioning of the State apparatus to such an extent that his very defiance would appear in the eyes of his supporters, if not the entire nation, as an act of liberation or even redemption when we see the profuse enthusiasm with which the United States' evangelical Christian right has welcomed Donald Trump. This is an enormous feat and the gamble seems so far to work in Trump's favor.

The most absurd and laughable manifestation of the appropriation of space is when newly arrived refugees from other lands are viciously and disdainfully treated by "Americans" whose families immigrated to this country only one or two generations before them. Statistics published after the election by the organization Edison Research showed that 54% of US Latino men voted for Trump in the 2024 election.[9] Blinded by their alienation as to the cause of their misfortune or by their supposed "success," they fail to see that it wasn't long ago when they (or their own family) were in the same boat.

Society, as Rousseau has pointed out, is corruptible, therefore the role of philosophy and poetry, and by extension of critical thinking, is to restore the integrity of the social being. What I come to understand and which has helped me a great deal in the appreciation of my existential journey, is that humans are more complex than we think when it comes to their relationship with Others, and that the stereotypes, the prejudices, the preconceived condemnations are all traps the sabotage the fulfillment of a liberated existence and collective mobilization

Finally, my poetry is a poetics of conscience, a poetics of outrage in the face of horrors. My poetry questions unfairness and injustice, and asks why this 22-year old male with mental challenges should sleep in a shopping cart, enveloped with heavy black plastic bags in the middle of Central Square in Cambridge? My poetry asks why this affluent society doesn't mind seeing humans in need become human debris lying down all along the Massachusetts Avenue? Why couldn't Harvard, MIT, Cambridge and Lesley colleges and universities give back to the community some small part of what they have taken from them?

Why can't they build a beautiful mansion along the Charles River on the Memorial Drive where the homeless people can feel safe to hang out, take a shower, perhaps be provided with counseling and learn a new trade? Why don't the real estate developers who've gained so much from this land lend a hand in making it a more beautiful and equitable place?

While poetry alone cannot provide the answer to such magnifying challenges, it can imagine, like philosophy, the hatching of the awareness of possibilities that exist, chief among them the possibility of building a genuinely humanist, democratic and egalitarian order—in the sense of equal socio-economic, cultural and educational rights and opportunities, equal protection under the law, and, ultimately, existential liberation.

It's always the same story, the twice-told tale: Could we one day craft a story based on the reality of everyday life, including the reality of the everlasting consequences of disastrous colonial conquests? The reality of the victims of socioeconomic disparities? This will require, one would surmise, a world order capable of making the perpetrators of human misfortune, even those placed at the highest level of the hierarchy of power, accountable to justice. This is certainly wishful thinking, but why not? Revolution is the collective faculty of thinking utopia.

I have difficulty grappling with the sort of alienation of the mind that makes people infatuated with the most gratuitous frivolities of life, at the expense of what Sartre calls transcendental categories, or Kant's ultimate moral imperatives. In this light, it's quite remarkable that in the Spring of 2024, after tens of thousands dead and all of Gaza in ruins, in the face of predatory gangs sowing terror in Port-au-Prince and elsewhere, in the midst of Russia escalating its aggression in Ukraine, the United States flirting with fascism, and democracy in danger; yes, it's remarkable that in the midst of so much misfortune at home and in the world, what a big chunk of public opinion in the US's cultural spheres cared the most about was the childish and tasteless controversy between the rappers Drake and Kendrick Lamar over their images!

Let us all hope one day that political poetry or poetry of consciousness would be given its due recognition as preeminent expression of intellectual manifestation of the soul. And not just narcissistic vociferations!

Poetry fails its magisterial role when it pretends that all is wonderful under the sky. There are more reasons to celebrate it when it challenges (through verses and personal *engagement*) the state of public affairs. There is something of great affective depth that happened to me after the destruction of Gaza and the subdued response of the European and the US politico-intellectual class: I now see almost everyone in this class as hypocrites—except of course the many brave combatants for justice and human liberation who have denounced the bellicose horrors in the name of a nobler conception of communal and national coexistence. Ultimately, only the marriage of poetry, philosophy, political praxis and collective mobilization can bring long term structural changes. The human project is always *en devenir*, in the making.

Finally, on my embrace of English

A few words now on my adoption of English. One of the greatest personal pleasures of my life has been my acquisition and embrace of the English language, a language that I grew to love despite my initial refusal to formally learn it during my first few years in the United States. A radical reaction to what I considered then as my forced exile from Haiti due to the US's support to the ineffective and murderous dictatorship of the Duvaliers. Quite fortunately, through my immersion in the life of this country, I became an admirer of the language's openness to flexible, descriptive conceptualization and creative daring, just like the Haitian language.

I am also lucky to have in my wife Jill Netchinsky—an excellent educator and poet in her own right—an editor who respects my well-guarded poetic license while not shying away from her role of guardian of the integrity of the English language! All my thanks, gratitude, and love to her. As I said in my other all-English poetry collection, *In the Beast's Alley* (2013), "I approach my writing in the English language as I do the preparation of a meal: I use the ingredients at my disposal to create an entirely new product... Writing in a language that I learned by necessity compelled me to create a new language, my language, the product of my *entendement,* of my own mind."

Finally, I like to play with words and concepts; I delight in their interaction, their resonance and dissonance. Despite the heart-wrenching nature of many of my poems' topics, I have felt great delectation for having been able to write them as well—besides Haitian and French—in English, this beautiful language.

My work remains committed to the same principles I formulated in the Introduction to *In the Beast's Alley:* "My poems want to reaffirm the notion that we are companions in the adventure of life, brothers, sisters, comrades, and fellow-travelers on life's journey. We are not natural enemies but, to the contrary, allies ineluctably bound in the great project of realization of a human society which supports a universal justice system that defends the rights of all and of each one of us. A society which preserves the qualitative integrity of a safe and livable ecologic environment, and which honors national self-determination for all; a society liberated from the mercantilist imperatives of capitalist corporations. A society liberated from hatred, exclusion, and exploitation of others. A society that reaches humanity."

—*Tontongi,* December 2024

Notes

1. For more on that notion, read my book, *Le Regard de l'Autre* (Tontongi, 2025), a collection of essays in French currently in final preparation.

2. I.C.E stands for Immigration and Customs Enforcement, the federal agency in charge of immigration control. It's possible that the acronym ICE was chosen because of its chilling effect!

3. See my poem "Climbing up Lady Liberty on a Fourth of July," dedicated to Therese Patricia Okoumou, the woman who climbed the Statue of Liberty in New York City in July 2018 to protest the treatment of migrants and immigrants by the Trump administration. The poem was published in the journals *Haïti Liberté* and *Tanbou*, in July 2018.

4. See my text «Chronique d'une fenêtre ouverte sur le règne du pseudo-Néron» (Chronicle of an Open Window Under the Rule of the Pseudo-Nero), in *Tyaka Poetica*, (Trilingual Press, 2021).

5. I wrote the last two paragraphs in 2019, that is under the first Trump administration, when no one was certain if the country would be able to sustain the Trumpian onslaught. I wanted to believe in the long view of History. Naturally, faced in 2024 with a new, and perhaps more worrisome, set of challenges presented by the fascist, totalitarian Project 2025, the country still needs to maintain its strength and fortitude.

6. This part of the Introduction is extracted from my text on the Haitian crisis "Haiti Has a Chance to Recover, Despite All Odds" published in the Spring 2024 issue of the journal *Tanbou*.

7. François Julien, *Si près, tout autre: De l'écart et de la rencontre* ["So Close and So Other: Of the Distance and the Encounter]. Our translation from the French (ed. Grasset, 2018), page 55.

8. See my poem "Haiti is Not What You Say, Mr. Tèt-Mato" published in the trilingual anthology *This Land, My Beloved*, (ed. Trilingual Press, 2023). Tèt-Mato means Hammer-Head, like the English "Blockhead".

9. Edison Research: "Latino Male Voters Shift Toward Trump in 2024," November 6, 2024: https://www.edisonresearch.com/latino-male-voters-shift-toward-trump-in4-election/

First Period Poetics

Poems of codification of memories and persevering heroic resistance by the people

A Word of Wisdom to the Disappointed Voters

After the glory days of 1789
Came Napoleon the butcher of freedom;
Then came the Restoration of the ancient régime.
After the parricide of the Pont Rouge in Haiti
Came two hundred years of oppression,
Then the hope of a better tomorrow.
After the valorous struggle and the sacrifices consented
By Tubman, Brown, Douglass and Lincoln to elevate
Our living together toward higher aims and decency,
Came Post-Reconstruction with its Jim Crow horrors.
After King's dream and Malcolm's defiance comes today
The nightmare of Trump inviting us to the abyss of hate.
Thus the circle continues but hope still remains alive;
History is a long journey of unknown turns.
Trump is today our turn and challenge,
The cries for hatred, exclusion and lynching
Will have passed as an aberration of the soul
If we counter them with our collective will
To building a better life and a wonder of being.
The Trumps and the Le Pens of our world
Are symptoms of expected madness to come.
Our endeavor is a betting on what is best in all of us.
Nightmares come and go still the day brightens,
The day to rejoice of our shared lives goes on.

A democratic election can go right or left
But the struggle for a better world is an on-going pursuit.
Our aspirations will remain
As long as our dreams live on;
Our days can be made of despair
And regrets and deceits that we're not proud of
But remember my friend, today will soon be gone,
But tomorrow will brighten a brand new day.
The struggle for a better life is our collective fate,
And life offers always an opportunity to reinvent our being.
We must not return to the darkness of years passed;
Our path to the beauty of being together remains illuminating.

(November 9, 2016)

Thought on a Blue and Red Weekend

Image of old white men rejoicing
glasses in hands in the White House
and happily cheering on the demise
of healthcare insurance for the poor
and for the disadvantaged among us
has made me sick and sad.
Some said they were playing cleverly
for their base's hunger for red meat,
others imputed them inner satisfaction
of hateful appetite for people's exclusion
outside the whole country they claimed
as only theirs with their pure living space
demonizing everything unlike them.

I feel bad living on the same planet
even being of the same species
as those who are so eager to bring forth
suffering to others in such cavalier manner
has if it didn't matter to them at all;
I feel ashamed for this point in our time.

Climbing up Lady Liberty on a Fourth of July

Dedicated to Therese Patricia Okoumou, the woman who climbed the Statue of Liberty in New York on the 4th of July 2018 to protest the treatment of migrants and immigrants by the Trump administration.

She has gotten her nerve, Therese,
from the millions who invaded the streets
on the past sunny Saturday of June.
Her wings have found solace
in the blowing wind of this Fourth of July
when she climbed up unabashed
the Statue of Liberty of all thing
to scream out her horrors
in the face of children put into cages
while their parents are thrown in jails.

She has gotten her nerve, Therese,
from the memory of all those
who died in the name of justice
and for higher avocation for this land.
She wants on this Independence Day
for Lady Liberty to be her witness
in exposing governmental atrocities.

She has gotten her nerve, Therese,
from those millions of consciences
on the last sunny Saturday of June
who called out the hypocrisy
of those who feign to incarnate
the most holy professed ideals.

She has gotten her nerve, Therese,
on this Fourth of July in pseudo Nero era
from those who take it to the streets
across the whole of the USA to say:
This land is all of ours!
No hate! No fear!
Immigrants are welcome here!

(July 4th, 2018)

I Heard the Voice of the Wife

Dedicated to Keith Scott, an African–American who was killed in Charlotte, North Carolina, on September 23, 2016, right in front of his wife Rakeyia Scott.

I heard her voice
direct as an intonation
imploring you not to kill
her husband without any judgment.
"It's the same old, my friend," I said,
the bartender and his friend concurred;
the same old impunity of power
the same structure erected though the ages,
Jim Crow version 21st century.
I heard her voice
impregnated of fore-sighting pain
telling you a human being was there,
a human with red blood and a conscience

From the left: **Danielle Legros Georges, Everett Hoagland, Askia Touré, Jill Netchinsky, Tontongi & Michel DeGraff in a poetry reading at the Out of the Blue Too Gallery in Cambridge**, Massachusetts, 2013.

and family and friends who would mourn
the odious act you intended to commit.

I heard her voice
but yours was the hell of death,
the blindness that covered the horrors,
yours was the silence of injustice.

I heard her voice
the agony of seeing the inevitable
unfolding like a horror movie,
the cry for you to listen to a voice
other than that of your fear and bigotry.

Tell me, how do you explain
that you no longer lynch the black man
on a tree in the light of the day
and still ambush him nights and days
and kill him scornfully like a rat?

Tell me, how do you invoke
ideals of civilization and rights,
rights of human beings to freedom
and yet let your police unrestrained
like hunting dogs in search of preys?
Those perhaps are bad apples blemishing good apples
but you let the bad apples kill without accountability
for the pain they have unnecessary caused.
Tell me, how do you let
the narrowness of your egoistic impulses
be elevated as normalized values?

(When killing is justified in war of conquest
it reverberates in the conqueror's back yard,
it penetrates his soul and the fiber of his brain
and all figment of his imagination;
it's the chain of macabre deeds
from General Barry McCaffrey
who killed with sadistic fervor
retreating Iraqi troops adhering to a cease-fire call
along the Highway of Death,
a carnage young Timothy McVeigh
had witnessed as an active actor sullied in blood and mayhem;
it had penetrated his soul and haunted his emotions,
the next thing we knew he blew up
in cavalier attitude and hubris
the Oklahoma City's Federal Building

where a great number of innocent people lost their lives.)
The culture of killing permeates all our senses
as symbiotic chemical elements in action;
it invades our doxa and ego as fetish and thrill.
You killed in the street not your fear
but a father or a son en route to their own endeavor;
you killed in the dark of the night or under the spotlight of our eyes
a human who had caused you no harm.

(The culture of killing mines your good old sense
manipulated as it is by MIIC's input
the Military-Informativo-Industrial Complex
oiled by wars and human suffering
and adds value to IRA's business boom
and security on-demand provided by Halliburton.
All parts of a diabolic chain of hurt, exclusion
and eco-degradation in a vicious circle only human action
can undo and reverse to give place to a better world.)

Yes, I heard her voice
forceful, direct, full of dignity,
telling you, telling us to stop your massacre
of black men's lives and aspirations.
"Don't shoot him, don't shoot him!", she pleaded,
"He didn't do anything," her voice intonated
in the silence interrupted by the fatal sound of the gun.
"He doesn't have a gun, he has a traumatic brain injury."
"Don't shoot him, don't shoot him!", she implored.
You killed because your cowardice
is nourished by hatred of the Other
whose gesture was seen as a threat.
You are so entrenched in yourself and shelve
you are ready to kill and cause pain.
Yes, black lives also matter as do all other lives!

Yes, I heard the voice of the wife
and also those of the protesters,
the voices of the brave women and men
of Fergusson, of Baltimore, of Charlotte
and all over the USA and the world
who are crying out loud that Black Lives Matter
demanding for justice to flourish
and for respect of all humans' rights and dignity.

(Cambridge, September 2016)

If You Think…

Dedicated to Michael Brown and Eric Garner

If you think America the beautiful
is no longer a race-baiting ugliness;
if you think killing a human being is a crime
when it is perpetrated by a killer cop;
if you think it doesn't matter
whether the victim is white, or brown or black;
if you think killing a human being is a crime
be it taking place in Ferguson, Staten Island, or LA;
if you think killing a human being is a crime,
think, think again, Brother.

If you think a black-faced presidential family
living in the White House is Black Power
or gives more rights to the excluded and the rejected;
if you think the adoration vested upon the Black Athletes
means they have evaded the auction block;
if you think Jim Crow was yesterday,
just as the lynching of the Ku Klux Klan
(by other means available)
and the forcing to the back of the bus
and the exclusionary zones
and the segregated schools
and the high unemployment unexplained
and the high representation in prison cells
and the relegation to sub-hygienic ghettoes
and the identification of the black man
with thief who reminds you to lock your car doors
and of the black-faced schoolboy to thug
thug to avoid at all price
and the deep sense of unfairness
and the self-loathing that leads to self-worthlessness;
if you think justice was done in Staten Island and in Ferguson
and all these places where black lives don't matter;
if you think Tamir Rice, Michael Brown, Jose (Kiko) Garcia,
Ernest Sayon, Nicholas Heyward Jr., Anthony Bacz,
Diallo, Patrick Dorismond, Ousmane Zongo,
Timothy Stansbury Jr., Sean Bell, Ramarley Graham,
Eric Garner, Akai Gurley,[1]
are just coincidences,
think, think again, Brother.

The victims' pierced bodies on the pavement
burst open the country's hypocrisy,
their death is a sad reality check
that reveals devilish hidden deeds;
their courage has enlightened the struggle
while their sacrifice is a donation
to the dream of building a new world, a space
where the Other is celebrated as a rightful being,
a beautiful part of a lovely Whole.

"I can't breathe! I can't breathe!" repeat
millions of protesters all over, "I can't breathe!"
just like the anti-Fascist poet called for «De l'air!», «De l'air!»
under Franco's universe of polluting fear.
"Black lives matter!" the protesters yell
all over the United States,
"Black lives matter!"
Human solidarity and brotherhood in action.
Black lives matter!
Though not all lives live the same agony
all lives matter as well;
they come today for the Blacks,
tomorrow they will come for YOU.

Misters and Misses of the Grand Jury
along with your masterful puppeteers,
you have perverted with your deed
the ideal of justice and fairness
you have upheld cultivated blindness
and reflexive reject as the compass of law and order,
your secretive decision all over
is infected with the smell of lie and deceit.
Had your dog been so cavalierly killed
by a zealous cop with high pumping adrenaline
you would certainly in earnest
seek retributive punishment for his death;
yet you have refused to a human being
the same caring regard you would allow your dog.

O poor human pity!
You don't deserve even despair
from those to whom you cause such a sadness
with your twisted judgment and bad faith.
May your memory live in infamy
for the rest of humans' quest for justice;
the struggle continues, so lives on our peoples'
craving for immanent justice and beauty!

Protesting is healthy and sound
injustice is such a horrible fate;
if killing here and there is OK
don't be surprised if the Bro blows your head;
let's stop all false justifications[2]
Circumstance has made these men a symbol
where they strived in their lives just to be;
if you think a State that condones execution-type killings
and militarizes its police resources to fight the people
is a State that protects your democratic rights,
think, think again Brother.

It's indeed rejuvenating to the soul
amidst global adoration of the self
within the grips of induced ignorance
to see the people's rage and togetherness,
in confronting Jim Crown Version 2014.

If you think all it takes is a good heart
that transcends the BS or a philanthropo-billionaire
that gives you tax money that makes him look happy,
happy modern emperor with deep pocket,
happy modern sorcerer with mediatic magic wand;
think, think again Brother.

If you think the Other is a Fanonian invention
with no correspondence in reality
if you think blackness and poverty
and bad schools and bad area codes
and no job attraction incentives
and jails that are full of Blacks and colored
and poor Whites lost in the American Dream,
sacrificial lamb to power and supremacy,
if you think you're not part of it, my friend,
think, think again Brother.

If you think white silence is not as hurtful as violence
if you think the oppressed is always subdued
and that you can play it by your own book;
if you think you are so powerful you can kill
as if you were the hand of God and Evil at once,
think, think again my friend,
think the cry of the people saying NO
the collective conscience calling for another way.

(December 4, 2014)

Notes

Gaze of Thunder

1. Names of Black men killed by police officers with impunity since 1990. The list was compiled by the *New York Times* of December 3rd, 2014 [Tamir Rice's name is added by us]: http://www.nytimes.com/interactive/2014/nyregion/fatal-police-encounters-in-new-york-city.html
2. This first part of the poem was written three weeks before an unstable Black man, Ismaaiyl Brinsley, cold-bloodedly gunned down in a Brooklyn, NY, street officers Wenjian and Rafael Ramos, claiming his unhappiness with the non-indictment of police officers involved in the killings of Michael Brown and Eric Garner. I wrote the following "Annex" poem to address those killings.

Annex to "If You Think…"

Yes, black lives matter
and blue lives matter too
so do all human lives
so does officer Wenjian Liu's life
so does officer Rafael Ramos's life
all human lives matter!
They all have mothers and sisters,
and fathers and sons and loved ones
who mourn their sudden departure;
they all have dug roots among the people
they have served or worked with

or went to church with when the clement sun

rendered their trip a little easier and pleasant.
These two may have joined the force pulled
by its claimed authority to serve justice well;
they may never have been destined
to kill in the dark of the night in cold blood

another human being even in the line of duty;
these deaths do not advance justice's pace.

But if you sow by way of the masterful use

of State-provided power and centuries-old legacies
and your grandpa's idolatries and connections
and his love for country and God to corrupt
our sense of what is fair and just and decent,
you darken the horizon of light with lies, and pains
that only exacerbate those who are already beaten,
and down, the circle is turning around, around,
until we brake it open, open

to let breathe new, fresh air.
"No justice! No Peace!" cry the protesters;
indeed where there is no justice
there is torment and sadness and pain
there is no value to human life.
No justice! No peace!

(December 26, 2014)

Remembering the Blizzards of 2015 in Boston

(A prose poem written from notes under the avalanche of snow)*

They came in series one after another with fury
and exhibited a calming potency that challenged time and space
reconditioning priorities while the air itself was re-purified,
all became white as the most beautiful of lilacs, pervading
life with its horrors and menaces, still exciting all the same
like in the *conte de fées*, but a fairy-tale of extremes,
extreme propulsion of wind, extreme propulsion of frothy
elements, Mother Nature imposing her limitless prowess,
and we the animal kingdom facing both tragedy and opportunity
lived the odyssey as we could, some of us even happy with guilt.

The first day of the first of the serial, terrifying storms,
I enjoyed their grandeur through the secured lenses of my windows;
the next day the bars were all open with exuberant attires,
and snowy romance regained attraction as the blizzards added zest,
and gained momentum and flourished, while the idyllic Nature-lover
turned to recriminations, for their job on the line, no longer
could the workers afford Nature's devastating caprices and ravages.

Within three weeks of the recurrent snowstorms they had deeply
tapped nerves not well-disposed toward them in the first place,
by now the white matter has become without any doubt the villain.
Amid such disdain for its supposed heavenly quality, I felt like a traitor
for loving the snow although I continued to exalt in its lacteal,
panoramic artistry, even when I was freezing on my way to the square.
The teeth-grinding noise of the blowing wind in the half silence of the night,
too beautiful to be really terrifying had somewhat appeased me,
"It's New England," I thought, until this snow blower's loud humming
polluted my quiet, and showered my face with high-powered, rapid
shooting of snow and blocking my view, I screamed "Hey! You!"
Nothing happened for a long instant, then suddenly the machine stopped
the operator had realized a human being was in peril.

The changed reality created a new, welcoming cordiality
among peoples of all creeds and races pushed by the narrowness
of the passageways to share spaces with genteel humanity.
The plow machines and their operators were the heroes du jour
battling the scourges of Nature with insistent devotion even
when the State allocation was meager and timid in the face
of angry MBTA passengers demanding accountability:
There was no love for the snow when stranded in traffic
for hours on end, hungry and tired after a ten-hour shift.

Many people just hibernated their cars leaving lines of snowy
monsters sculpted by Nature's capricious sense of order and beauty.
The most caring of the residents and businesses did a great job
cleaning up the sidewalks, others just complied with the law's minimum
standard and other just didn't give a damn, like Phil's Towing
who left its sidewalk untouched by any human consideration or caring
even after making big bucks towing people's cars with frenetic zeal.
Those gave the pedestrians the choice between climbing up piles of snow
or subject to getting killed by drivers frustrated
by the slow pace of things.

We ought to negotiate every instant of survival and challenge our
worst bestial instincts, often having to *re-deal* the whole house of cards,
bring about new guiding principles emanated from the simple
principle
just to be there, there, among other elements that Nature oppresses.

And just like the last spasm of the white liquid ending with hurrah
its feisty adventure, the Blizzards gave a finale befitting their grandeur;
they blanketed the aging piles of darkened and dirty snow with new,
virginal, fluffy snow that danced in unison with the brightening sun
—the horizon had become a piece of art, an enlivening beauty.
I remember how immense a pleasure I took as a rebellious boy
when I witnessed the devastating fury and terror of Hurricane Flora
ravaging my beloved Port-au-Prince—I enjoyed her daring challenge
to Papa Doc's order of things, the blow to his claim of absolute power!

The Blizzards of 2015 gave humility lessons of their own,
they taught us that human legs, besides their playful quality are
the most reliable means of transportation, and even of well-being.
They also told me that whatever else had or could have happened
in the world, or whatever other news that CNN would broadcast,
people's awareness was blurred by the immediate tragedy
that they were confronting in the moment which captured
their attention, and their sense of humor.
I overheard many secret uses of the storms' redefinition
of space and comfort and all; some welcomed the freedom
they provided to be lazy and feel the moment, expressing
the hope they'd help them have long overdue babies,
while others lamented their loneliness although snow romances
had suddenly quadrupled even in the cold.
Poised to confront the Blizzards' onslaught with exciting apprehension
Jill cooked a large pot of soup made of split peas and sausage
as I made rice and beans to sweeten our forced retreat.
Deep in my inner soul even in the face of people's frustrations
and unmet expectations, I delighted in the sudden change of rhythm,

in the diminished functionality of normality the Blizzards had imposed;
they regained majesty in my eyes
—even when unsure of their ultimate intent.
The people found ways by sheer will power and the fear
of losing their jobs or their high living comfort to cope,
with ingenious calm, with this thing—this white thing all over
had brightened perceptions and even the most goody-goody
of the citizens questioned the State Administration's
lack of imagination and preparedness although
no one could predict Nature's fury and capricious
malevolent impulses on such long a duration.
It's New England indeed, we knew in this place on Earth
all can happen at once, and all four seasons and their extremes
can cohabit within half of an afternoon as naturally as possible
as if that were their normal occurrence.
The Blizzards of 2015 won the battle
but they will have faded away in our memories;
hopefully this poem will be a testimony to their glory.

(2015)

> *This poem was also published in CHA's magazine, *Auxcultations,* Cambridge, MA, 2015.

From the left: **Anna Salamone, Aldo Tambellini, Brenda Walcott, Askia Touré & Tontongi at Walcott's birthday party in her courtyard in Cambridge**, Massachusetts, in 2016.

The Causalities of Evil

Part I: The Masters of Quake Land

Dedicated to the victims of Haiti's 2010 Earthquake

They lay in wait on the bridge
called Pont Rouge like the blood
on that sweaty October night,
Défilé the Crazy unceremoniously put
the Emperor's remains in a more dignified place.
The vermin that followed this round
brought terror wrapped as salvation
thus completing in the believers' eyes
the reverend Robertson's divine wrath.

It's the conspiracy of the oil industry
in league with Bord-de-mer exploiters
Grand dons and ambitious politicians
to deplete the land for City Bank of New York.[1]

We held the hope in the year of the quake
that tragedy could portend better days
even though certain signs of bad faith
would plead vividly for the contrary.

It is not God's job to bring forth punishment

upon a land cursed by others' evil deeds
nor is the prayer of the sacristan
the citizens' sole last words.
Nor could quakes, serial coups d'etat
even assassinations of emperors and presidents
undo the original sin of slavery and conquest
through mayhem, subjugation, and faith.

Haiti was born in the name of freedom
and continues to pay for choosing that road;
already Charles X sent fourteen ugly warships
to the Port-au-Prince shore, demanding remittance
for supposed property lost by slave masters!
That ransom was the first quake from Paris
overrun by the Ancien Régime's false
splendor, flooded in arrogance of power.
Nature wants to teach us the wrong tale,
she chooses the wrong targets and culprits,
these are innocent prey of the same predators.
What about the oil magnates and Wall Street?
the lazy financiers, the sumptuous emirates,
the uncaring bourgeois lost in their neuroses
who supported your villainy with hubris
What will their chastisement be?
How could Rumsfeld die in his sleep?
The US has chosen the moronic QAnon path
instead of all the values it pretends to stand for,
human rights, democratic ideals, justice, and equity
are thrown into the sewers of Jim Crow nostalgia.

No one is innocent on the part of the Earth
made of heroes and lovers of freedom,
and also of jackals and spurious angels
who blew a presidential palace with no qualms
with family and children, and everyone inside.
Who could have set such an awful explosion?[2]
Here, lies and illusions by unrepentant bourgeois
are made sacred revelations, and cause for jubilation

Underdevelopment, like degradation,
is a process that stems from long-endured
malfeasance and thievery culminating over
centuries-old evil deeds and madness.
The tectonic fault lines are many,
the universe playing ball with our destinies.
May new generations help forge,

here and everywhere, a new path
toward an inclusive communality,
and build a space of love and care,
a center of beauty to marvel at ease,
even on the darker side of the sun.

Notes

1. Following the U.S. occupation of Haiti in 1915, the debt servicing of the French-imposed, crippling Independence indemnity was transferred to the National City Bank of New York, an American bank (since renamed CitiBank).
2. On August 8th 1912, the Haitian National Palace was blown up by a powder explosion that killed 400 people including the President of the republic, Gen. Cincinnatus Leconte, according to the *New York Times*.

Part II: The Intersection of Suffering and Resistance

Dedicated to Van Hardy

Slave hunters on horseback
cavalierly aiming the lasso
moving like owners of stolen lands,
this time it's the Rio Grande,
reminiscent of bygone Wild West conquest,
mayhem, rape, and torture
of other inhabitants of the land;
yes, just like yesterday.

Yes, Thomas Jefferson,
you strangled Haiti's dream
with your 58-year embargo
against the newly free, rebellious
Maroons resisting France's rule,
their struggle helped the United States
acquire lucrative new Gulf States,
doubling the future Empire's living space[1].

Yes, you, Woodrow Wilson,
blemished the Haitian people's hopes
with your sacrilegious violation
of Jean-Jacques Dessalines' resting place.
O land of freedom becoming land to flee from!

Mass deportations in the 21st century, like sheep
unknowingly en route to the slaughterhouse
handled with no process nor care;
revived flutters of the earthquakes' horrors
when beautiful bodies grabbed like rubbish
were thrown in the common pit.

While the Mayflower was welcomed
with gifts of knowledge, flowers and food,
you bring up your hateful, violent cowboys,
as if chasing vultures on a vast savanna
and not suffering and sanguine human beings;
what a horrible sight
what a failure of empathy!

It's a causality chain of calamities
and a correlation of malfeasance;
it's the failure of a whole state of things.
It's certainly hard to explain the despair
that makes people brave

many adversarial horrors
and misfortunes paving their way
to find a better life, to achieve
a more decent condition of existing.

It's the causality that establishes
and nurtures a thuggish State
and permits it to prosper
on the south flank of paradise.

It's the Columbus reflex in reverse,
the repelling trajectory,
Haiti the beautiful
turned a hellish and menacing enclave
amid dictators, tonton-macoutes,
corrupt *débrouillards* state minions,
kidnappers in dark alleys
Bourgeois sans conscience
and neocolonials from overseas.

It's the end-product of dreams
based on Bon Papa taking charge
of all your problems and aspirations;
the fall-out from the voracity
of the Haitian Big Eater class,
those jackals who don't mind the dirt roads
along their mansions made on foreign soils.
Those who aligned themselves with evils
to keep the populace under control.

It is the political causality
blended in oppression
revamped by exclusion
that neither Biden nor Obama
nor Trump could fully comprehend,
they who deported by the thousands
the refugees from lost lands.

The causalities of evil
and their many facets
involve the intersection
of suffering and resisting.

A system that kills
and rationalizes it away
as a narrative of Barbarians
invading and destroying properties

is the same that beats up refugees
at the borders and elsewhere.

Barbaric is the Wisconsin state law
allowing earnestly for judge and jury
to be chosen à la carte
just to let a killer go
and get way with murders[2].
It is the same transatlantic causation
the one that brought people
like produce and sheep to the marketplace;
the same interwoven determinants
waving across the Andes,
through the Caribbean or the Pacific
that compress life's flow
within the confines of greed,
a vision to dominate,
to pacify,
to wipe out the Other.

The causalities of evil
bring about the resistance
of alterity leading the battle
for human sublimity.

It's the same people
at governance
or head of board
the same gentrifying machine
that throws whole neighborhoods
into turmoil and hardship,
re-zoning as a tool for an Others-free zone.

It is the vision of Van Hardy
and the brothers and sisters of Union United
Somervillians of heart and nerve
along with Books of Hope,
the Media Center in the middle of the square
and the Welcome Project
embracing newcomers
from many continents
from many perimeters of pain,
using their praxis
in the name of beauty.

Yes, this is beauty,
the knock on the doors

to reveal to the neighbors' consciousness
misdeeds done in their names.
Yes, it's the constellation of hope,
a vocation to have the struggle serve
as a long march to expand the horizon,
spread the wealth for the betterment of all,
the fulfillment and always revealing
quest for justice and decency
the pursuit of the pleasure in living.

Yes, solidarity with all wretched of the Earth!
Asylum for all the refugees!
May we join together to undo the causalities of evil!

(November 27, 2021)

Notes

1. Because of his defeat in Saint Domingue (the name the French gave Haiti) by the Black rebel armies of Toussaint and Dessalines, Napoléon Bonaparte was compelled to sell the French Louisiana territories to the United States in order to finance his war against England. The Louisiana Purchase, as it became known, extended United States sovereignty across the Mississippi River, nearly doubling the size of the country. The purchase included land from fifteen current U.S. states and two Canadian provinces.

2. Allusion to the acquittal verdict of Kyle Rittenhouse on November 19, 2021, for killing two white men, and badly wounding a third who came to support a Black Lives Matter demonstration in Kenosha, Wisconsin.

From the left: **Denizé Lauture, Jeanie Bogart, Tontongi & Charlot** at the HCE's sponsored reading of the trilingual anthology **"This Land, My Beloved"** at the Center for Fiction, in Brooklyn, New York, on June 16, 2024.

From the left: **Franck Laraque, Tontongi & Paul Laraque** in the latter's apartment in Queens, New York, in 2004.

The Business of Saving Lives

Dedicated to the victims of the Las Vegas massacre in 2017

Amidst our busy workload
challenging the curse of human illnesses
we found time to afford a night out,
a lovely get together of colleagues
enjoying rare moments of leisure,
laughter, and laissez-faire flippancy,
symbiotic team spirit
under the season's generous charm
playing along with life's cadence
after giving much unconditional love
and human empathy for duress
during a long week of trial and effort;
such a pleasure it is to be alive and well
on this beautiful Earth of ours.

Our choices are multidimensional,
carved in the perimeter of being,
the instant could become either a dead end
or an eternal exploration of space
or the joyful and painful journeys
experienced throughout our living;
will you make of it a beauty or an agony?

We are in the business of saving lives
and bringing smiles to faces ravaged by pain
more reasons we lament all killings of humans
be they perpetrated in our names or our greed
or for the twisted pleasure of an unrestrained ego.

We save even the killers' lives when we can,
still we place in the same basket of horrors
killing for the honor of the Fatherland
in the middle of battle on vast lands
animated by fear and the fervor of the flag,
and the killing by drones from afar
while sitting in an air-conditioned crib
detached from the nuisance of human emotion;
yet we watch others benefit from the darkness,
while the barbarians have ever more guns.

How can we let people die of neglect
within the plenitude of waste?
Why can't we harvest what is best

of ourselves minus the jackals of all stripes
and remake our world
in the image of justice and love?

I recollect January 21st, 2017,
the immense ocean of people
joining hands to reject the poison
that was offered as redemption;
their foresight proved so right
even in the distance of time.
In the face of democraticide
and menace on all fronts
resistance is our most precious means
to uphold our values and ideals.

We are torn between many loves
and conflicting choices that can be
unified in transcendental solidarity.
My friend, we should continue to dance,
even in the absence of music and song.

Between the unknown of the next instant
and the overlapping of the past and present,
the evolutionary process never stops,
nor do the occasions to despair;
still also exist moments to rejoice
and bring about ample new beginnings;
the covenant to reach beauty
can be achieved in due time.

Let's all choose the long course of wisdom
over the narrow-mindedness of the instant.
I'm looking forward to the next full moon
penetrating the spellbinding calm
of a New England Fall night.

(October 2017)

The Children at Aganman's Gate[1]

Horrified and crying
in sudden appearance
at Aganman's gate
the children take refuge in their tears
to appease their sadness.

They were told that the long journey
toward the vast Unknown
while not made of roses
would end in a marvelous feast.

The children didn't know a thing
about Versailles, Berlin, Hiroshima,
and not even nearby Guantanamo.
even less about Afghanistan,
Iraq or Syria, Gehenna enclaves
where the killers' dance has no end.
The children were told at the end
their amiable Uncle from the North
would be there with his charming

embrace to welcome them with joy;
they didn't know that our world
could be such a mean place.
They did not know that Auschwitz
would be less of a memory
than a continual menace
to those still dreaming of freedom.
They could not know,
that the parental warmth
experienced until then
would be ending so soon.
The children's cry is the cry of silence
made recluse behind closed doors;
they're sending us echoes of the kind
of pain felt when giving life to them;
their cry exposed what was supposed
to be faded away incognito,
in the never-happened ethereal world.
Their cry is a verdict

against pretending otherwise,
their cry compels us to ask
what happened to Mom and Dad,
and how come they are not there with them?

Why their voice is not heard
by those with such power to hurt?

Their cry implores us to inquire
about what happened to their childhood,
to their innocence once made sacrosanct
in moral manuals sold to the converted?
How come their land turned out to be yours
and the Rio Grande where their ancestors
washed their clothes are still awash in blood?

The children didn't know that
the land was never yours from the start;
they didn't know that it could ever exist
among us such a glacial universe
nor if the Sun would for sure
escape climate change.

The children didn't know that
you made it possible to mass arrest
thousands of people in one day
and cage them and their children
like animals farm in hellish,
tender-age concentration camps?
How could the children know
that hatred and killing
are being normalized
since five hundred years ago?
The children didn't know
that silence is consent in disguise
and that the process is made
to be heartless as an angry shark;
they didn't know that, how could they?
The children didn't anticipate
that horrors would be part of the scene,
they didn't know that you wanted
an unjust society as your spoil.

The children didn't know we could be
such willing and consensual sheep
to this emotionless specter that threatens
our lives through cultivation of our greed.

The children didn't know we can also
elevate our moments of togetherness
toward aspirations and positive energies
that enhance the everyday meaning of living.

The children didn't know
—how could they?—
that assholes exist everywhere
and that if we fight for what is right
there's a chance to make a difference.

(June 20, 2018)

   1. *Aganman* is an evil being in Haitian mythology.

The Dead Boy on the Beach

Dedicated to the Middle East Refugees and the Haitian-Dominican Deported

The dead boy on the beach
swamped by the ocean's waves
his body lay along the windy beach
is a reminder of your deeds and bad faith;
he is the fruit of your labor
he is a reminder of what was done
years before he was even conceived
years before the Libya's no-fly-zone
years before Kuwait was declared liberated.

The dead boy on the beach
and his older brother and mother
and thousands others who cross the seas
and perished and eaten by the sharks
are the harvest of what you have sowed.

The dead boy on the beach
his father mortified, dejected by his losses
is the product of your stratagems
the byproduct of power that makes and
dismantles, holding in your hands and hubris
destinies of whole communities,
mastering the science of control and subjugation.

The dead boy on the beach
along with the Haitian-Dominican deported
from the land of their birth
thrown out to the unknown
their odyssey is a testimony of our defeat
defeat of human decency
defeat of the spirit of solidarity.

The dead boy on the beach
is what happens when DR's actions
are not counteracted by the world conscience
letting people to be thrown to a land of suffering
that is facing its own challenge to horrors,
its own challenge to the accomplices of DR's madness.

The dead boy on the beach
is the spin-off of Benghazi in flame
when a dictator's demise was traded
as dividend shares at the Stock Market
exemplar of what destruction can achieve

symbol of power projected from the sky
coalition of the sages with money and missiles.

The dead boy on the beach
and his companions in human hell
from the Levant as from the Caribbean
are reminders of what happens
when crazies are given free reign
in matters of life and death.

The dead boy on the beach
is what happens when State power goes unrestrained
what happens when religion is the guide
and combines with greed and xenophobia
to create even more marvelous Gehenna.

The dead boy on the beach
is not a social media sensation;
he incarnates the cruel truth of degradation
the dreadful non-poetry of his death

is no accident, nor an isolated case;
it's the implementation of data analysis
the component of cosmological scheme
only a world wide counter-scheme can defeat.

The memory of this dead boy,

laying on the beach
is the history of things passed,
the happening faded in absence
human contingence in action.

Tell my why the dream of a better world
shared by all refugees on Earth
must be a scourge and not a grand embrace,

an osmosis of destinies
refined to the image of our dreams,
immanence as the order of things,
beauty made expression of what is real
the reach of the Other as transcendent
in a world perverted by blind faiths
leading little minions to their celebrated hell…
O beautiful hell!

The dead boy on the beach
bellies a wrong way on the road
the signal to take the right turn.

(September 2015)

The Emperor's Last Speech

Watching Donald Trump's first address to the Congress on February 28, 2017

As the date attests, I wrote the following poem soon after Trump's first State of the Union speech on February 28, 2017. Given everything that was said about him then and the prospect of impeachment, I really thought this one could be his last speech—I was thinking of course in terms of a normal country.

Necessity makes the man,
we said back in the old country;
a huge meteoric onslaught
is coming his way the signs show,
and his speech's imperial tone
carried the night for the court's Gallery.

The ritual was a perfect Valium
for everyone these past long weeks
trapped in the sadomasochist roller-coaster
of manufactured crises à la Steve Bannon
to bring about nirvanaesque elation
for the "deconstruction of the administrative State."[1]

The Emperor indeed had clothes that night,
his great night brimming in the spotlight
of the fatherland, and the herd applauding
and looking around for recognition,
inhaling the smell of power.

He had a tough few weeks, the Emperor,
his mastery gaming of facts and reality,
and his mixing them with the Ether World
has taken a blow from the "people's enemy.[2]
A part of me salutes that witty scamming
of materialistic essence of Void and Nothingness,
although Void with financial prowess.

The decorum was a perfect hiding
shield for such a tormented soul
that even Hell itself might refuse.
And yet I salute him for having gained power
not through the Establishment's shoulders
as had his loving-hating buddy the Kenyan,[3]
but through the debasement of the all tribe;
I salute his courage to resist virtue.
Necessity makes the man, we said.
The Emperor accomplished more

than even he ever thought his privileges
would afford him in normal circumstances.
"If I could do that, I can do this,"
he is now saying, caged in the spiral
of high crimes and misdemeanors and system's
malady that haunts his every day's living;
the Emperor might as well prefer to be happy
in his past private world instead of this mess.
The Emperor knows how to use
his voice to project power,
his greed to inspire emulation and envy,
his daredevilness to instill fear:
Does he know how to survive in earnest
two congressional and FBI investigations?
a pile-up of enemies on Day D?
Rubio and Cruz and Christie taking revenge?
Flynn talking to the feds?
his fast friends on the Hill panicking like chicken?

I thought that I hated his guts
and braggartism, then he said
in the middle of a Washington DC street
that NATO is obsolete and unneeded,
many of us almost warmed to his charm;
then he said, "I hate you all suckers!"
I almost thought that I would miss
a Ku Klux Klan denier, a birther founder[4]
and Central Park black teenagers' accuser
for his candid epicture of his cast.
Is the Emperor more than a TV clip?
More than his bulliness and posture?
More than what looks like shadow?
He has hurt too many people
to be exempted of destiny's redress;
his fate will just be justice done
in the name of Earth's higher aim.
One doesn't in impunity destroy
society's simple decency and ethics;
the Emperor missed this original meaning,
and that was the cause of his demise.
The day after his speech to the Imperial Gallery
all was back as usual to the drip-drip bleeding;
it then turned out like in an Opera's twist
his Minister of Injustice indeed had with
the All-Eyes-Great Empire from the East,

as did the Emperor's son-in-law and a plethora
of fake double-agents and avid sycophants,
and all the amateurs of this série noire movie
acting under the guidance of the Commissar.

My heart bleeds for the refugees, the migrants
escaping horrors of civil strife and war of domination;
my heart bleeds for the exploited, underpaid
undocumented workers entangled in the trap
tended by the Emperor's ICE.[5]
My heart is saddened for the people
of this great land of hope and revival.
May the probity that guided it in the past
still illuminate the path to tomorrow.
State affairs are no comedy nor game
—real people suffer everyday in silence
on the other side of the spotlight.
May the Republic's ideals save the day,
may human kindness survive this debasement
of our values and all that is dear to us;
may the madness of the privileged cast
be a simple asterisk of horror.
There's more to life than appearance,
also exists the nudity of the poignant instant,
hope busted in the ashes of the non-event,
the Other lost in an inescapable jungle.

Necessity makes the man, we said,
many centuries of searching for liberation
of the soul from the regimen of the plantation,
from the factory's conditioning of space,
from the Military's impulse to control and kill,
from society's measurement of what counts,
shouldn't last in a moment of folly and caprice.

The Emperor's first speech was his last word,
scripted in the well-behaving teleprompter,
it was his only real claim to glory in this land
of fast passing forgetfulness and remembrance.
The Emperor's fate will be well deserved
as that of all tyrannies in the world;
still I will miss his hubris and motherfuckerness.

The Emperor had said to his pal
"Why do you think we are so innocent?"
such utterance enhances his appeal,

for once he tells his people the truth
about this land he surely knows so well
—this is one more reason we'll miss the Emperor.

(And a few days later, early in the morning,
he sounded the alarm that he was illegally surveilled
by his non-American, Kenyan predecessor. Nobody,
or only just a few believed him this time around
—he was now proved a person whose words
one cannot trust, he now joined the twilight pathway
between the crazy demagogue and the calculating idiot).

The Emperor may go or stay
but life here will never be the same;
he may choose to retreat to Mar-a-Lago[6]
early in the morning after a last tweet;
he may decide to wonder around
like the amusing ghost of the town,
still we all should ask every day
he's out there tweeting and all
what is really up with him?
The Emperor is real
as are his artifices and antics,
as are the sufferings of the people.
His shielding behind his fake common feel
cannot absolve his unleashing of hatred and fear.
We will have passed as a simple memory of time
if we fail to grasp what societal madness
looks like in real time.

(March 3rd 2017)

Notes

1. Quoted from a statement by Steve Bannon, Trump's principal advisor, at the CPAC conference on Feb. 23, 2017.
2. Trump has called the US national press "the enemy of the people."
3. In reference to Barack Obama that Trump accused of being Kenyan and not American.
4. Trump for years had insisted that Barack Obama produce his birth certificate to prove that he was born in the United States. This demand and the people who believe in its premise constitute what that has been called the "birther movement."
5. ICE: Immigration Control Enforcement, the federal agency in charge immigration, and thus, of the repression and deportation of the un-documented.
6. Mar-a-Lago is Donald Trump's personal residence in Florida.

From the left: **Tontongi, Askia Touré, Richard Cambridge & Patricia Frisella** at the Poetry Festival in New Hampshire in 2016.

The Long March From Charlottesville to Boston

Charlottesville was the event,
the catalytic boom
to say «braham di sètase!»
Abraham says: Enough is enough,
like the Haitians said in 1791
when they threw the slave-masters out;
enough of the demonization
of the other side of yourself!
Enough of your self-imposed
myopia that further narrows the road to the abyss
of the darkest part of us.
Enough of your refusal to admit
that the world is not reduced to you
nor to the mirror of your clan.
We need a huge constellation,
of consciences en éveil, awakening
just like some of our brave ancestors
had fought to save this land,
the land that is still struggling to redeem
its horrible past and misdeeds.
If we must march, we will
to defeat at whatever cost it might take
the distortion of life you so eagerly
promote for your own selfish gain.

Boston had held high the torch
on that day when 40,000 resistants
claimed the Common as theirs.
"Silence is violence," said one sign,
others extol the sanctity of life,
"Black Lives Matter" people yelled,
yes, indeed, Black lives matter too,
despite what the police's gun would imply.
In the face of so many lives
of black men and women all over
destroyed in the absurdity of evil,
Boston has held high the torch
not that of hate and white supremacy
but that of love espoused by Dick Gregory
a great soul who sadly passed away
only a couple of days after the great rally;
he had made the agitation for civil rights
a movement of love and brotherhood
where our aspirations for change
always were on the line;
I see him again, impetuous rebel
his face beaming with hope
in so many marches in DC.

Boston has held high the torch
the torch of togetherness the torch of solidarity
brighten in all our peoples' faces
made of all shapes and shades;
it was a beautiful day in Boston, indeed.

No passaran! No KKK!
No Trump! No Fascist USA!
We chased away those souls lost
in the nothingness of rejection
of others and themselves;
we wanted to celebrate life
with all its flavors and uphold
our vision toward higher wonders.
The human chain on the Boston Common
invited even policemen on duty to join them
in the fervor and cry together "Boston Strong"
—Boston was strong indeed against hate.
The unrelenting protesters on that sunny day
enliven in the purple color of Heather Heyer
forced the Nazis to skulk away like chicken,

overwhelmed by the human ocean
defiant and ready to swallow them;
the valiant and lovely person she was
would not have died in vain
—she knew nothing is settled forever
and that the cycle of hate always returns
even among those hurt by oppression's disdain.
The Boston marchers marched
on this sunny, refreshing Saturday
amid the many faces of beauty
and the energizing human warmth
also to reject alienation and horrors
thrusted upon disempowered human beings
crushed by corporate greed of those
for whom outsourcing people's jobs
and lives is just sportive exercise,
while worries to pay bills
is a failing of character;
their suffering is being used
to change them to monsters
lurking around with their resentment
in the jungle of life and all
—Heater Heyer also died for their cause.
Statues are just symbols of the past,
we need those that unite and celebrate
our common fate and uncertain future
in defiance of evil:
the marchers of Boston have shown the light.
I saw a country in mourning
on that night of infamy
when truth slipped away
from the neo-Nero's mouth.
On many faces of grown men and women,
black, white, yellow, and of all creeds
I saw tears and the people's sorrow;
I saw the tears of past glory
on the battlefield of the fight
for human decency and dignity.
The tears lamented the great harm
to the US' ideals we are all witnessing
along with all the sycophants in Nero's place
intent on shedding tears at all cost.
They shall be resisted with the torrent
of vast human rebellion to bring a simple taste of life
in the grotesque universe of hate.

We are all Charlottesville
joining the grand forum
to end the tunnel of ignorance.

Boston again has been the cradle
for the collective conscience to say no:
No to the abyss of darkness
Boston had redeemed Charlottesville
on that day even though we had our share
of a few bad apples among those
whose duty is to protect us all.
Boston was the conscience of the land,
it has said no KKK!
No Trump! No Fascist USA!

(August 20th, 2017)

The Panhandler

By the coffee shop entrance door
she stood animatedly panhandling,
gaze battered by the indignity
of such venture of last resort.

Unlike traditional practitioners
who used catchy phrases like
"Can you spare some change?"
this one, unperturbed, elaborated
a long, introductory prelude
mixing words like "hunger" and "need,"
to justify the request
and the urgency to give handsomely.

Some patrons hesitated, listened,
then moved away with shameless candor;
some others just passed her by,
unmoved by the panhandler's call.

From my standpoint of scrutiny
I felt she was wasting her time
and wished she would cut her losses
and her lengthy plea to the chase.

Then came a forty-something woman
to the shop, less concerned
by the challenge to her entrance;
upon listening to the panhandler's
long litany, she offered to pay her lunch,
thus they entered the coffee shop,
friendly and happy
as if winners of a long battle.

Waiting in the cashier's line
a friendly little girl
unbridled and unabashed
by the attention of grown-ups
asked the panhandler
as if the most natural thing to do
to give her the cookie she was about to buy.

Upon securing with her eyes
the child's mother's approval,
the panhandler gave her the cookie
with a smile, and the smile was shared
by all the patrons of the coffee.

In this moment of apprehension,
the country's past and present
coalesced in an ugly chemistry
of the meanest of measures
in an implacable agreement
between the elements of the power structure
to ignore the pain and suffering caused
to those born without a silver spoon,
the panhandler had saved the day.

Though victimized
by their machination
to making scarcity
the eleventh Commandment,
the panhandler became beauty
personified in the face of the ugliness
of things joined together
in a Cambridge's busy street
—perhaps the remade land

Like a Genet character transformed
from the most sullied of society's rejects
to become the most sublime of artists,
the panhandler was elevated to divine status
for having dismissed the communication wall
erected to separate our human species.

After the lunch
the panhandler retreated
with her dignity intact
to the anonymous nature
of her world and life:
"Free at last!" she now thought,
even in this unsettling time in the USA.

(May 2017)

From the left: **Askia Touré, Tontongi, Neil Callender, Aldo Tambellini, and Gary Hicks** (seated) at a poetry reading in Cambridge, Massachusetts, in 2013—*photo by Tony Melenik Van der Meer.*

On Giving
We all like the person
who gives with a nice smile
smoothed in tenderness
something that enlivens your life;
it could be a free drink on a tight night
or refusing money for a favor,
something that infuses you
with a sense of togetherness;
there's something sexy about giving,
especially on a slow night
—just the way you felt
the last time you gave.
(Avril 29th, 2017)

Terrorism of the Mind

Dedicated to Mahmoud Darwish, the great Palestinian poet

[For nearly a month, from July 8 to August 5, 2014, Israel launched a continuous, systematic, ferocious attack on the Gaza Strip, killing 1,900 people, 80% of them civilians, including a large number of children. The number of wounded exceeds 9,000 according to the United Nations. The destruction caused by the offensive is hellish, the infrastructure of the city mostly devastated. Total suffering. The scale of the aggression indisputably qualifies it as a crime against humanity for which Israel must be prosecuted and punished. This poem is inspired by that tragedy.]

It makes truth a sacred Un-said
and silence a virtue like civism and brunt
force, right hand of security imperatives
and other bullshities and vaudevilleries
that keep life from spreading.

It's the rigidity of the Cosmos, they say,
the Bible announced it some time ago
so did the Torah, the missiles and the Iron Dom
which grabs the Hamas' rockets from the sky
and everything. I'm choking! I'm choking!

With your Patriot Batteries deviators of terror
and your armored tanks blowing death everywhere
with your great eloquent voices at Harvard
with your huge investments at Wall Street and London
with your alliance with the world's Unique Superpower
who hovers over our heads like a furious eagle,
like an enveloping shadow, fluid, atmospheric;
with your great technological prowess
stunning like a thunderstorm's carnival;
with your AIPAC's sponsored symposiums[1]
and the luminaries who are welcoming you as Providence
while you are piecing Gaza like Swiss cheese
and the diversion of the water toward just your village
with your great accomplishments
and your golden medals, your architecture
of enclosure—the Panopticon
that closes on the Mediterranean Sea—,
with all the honors Destiny has blessed you,
still you're killing innocent children
and driving many widows to poverty.

It makes of decency an unknown entity

and of conscience a no man's land
it dictates the march of the process
of peace and war
and the Re-beginning
perfect like the recurrence of the seasons,
the hospitals, the maimed, the flattened villages
are something else. Your illusion.

It's clamoring to your ears
terrorist alerts that keep you from sleeping
ISIS has vindicated them, they say,[2]
It's the prophecy of a well-informed oracle.
We can even love each other, I know
but this is not a game, you know?

And even our pain and cries
our lavish blood flowing under the debris
the victorious wars you had launched
couldn't stop your voracity for glory, they say,
still you are killing children
and sending your undesirable Others to agony.

You have the power to distort logics
and you use it with marvelous results,
even our tears, they say, are being served
to reach higher aim for your people while
you debased our people without any remorse.
Just like storms and tornadoes
you destroy life at will and throw
half of the nation to the street, while
on the other side of the wall
you are lighting in splendor
your bombs raining like celebratory sparks
on Gaza dimming in the dark.

You have the God-blessed power
to keep the eyes from seeing the horrors
and the ears from hearing the wailings
and the mouth from speaking loudly,
still you are killing children in broad daylight.

I am ashamed of my contemporaries, coward
zombies of farms and streetwise opportunists
alienated by the conditioning of a securized soul,
you let our daughters disappear, raped and sold
you pretend to have condemned Bush's Iraq adventure
while you praise the Obama-Nantanayu-Gaza-pact.

You have made of evil a daily routine that bothers
no one certainly not the arms dealer
nor the corner McDonald, of course not.

It makes you a coward CNN reporter
a misleader from MSNBC who condemned Rula Jebreal
for having said loudly what everyone whispered;[3]
it makes you a falsely objective State minion,
it returns you to the state of pure humanity
dirty fleshly cadaver living for the moment,
it returns you to the sanitary state that refuses
to be contaminated by knowledge.

With the ambient threat, your job on the line
the chastisement of exclusion, the contemplation
of homelessness' Gehenna, the reflex self-regulates,
you have too much to lose now.

Ah! These non-Christian little kids,
may their death serve to defeat the local terrorist
the self-justification obeys the rule
evilness is the attribute of goodness
—and the debate is closed, let's talk about Ukraine
and the World Cup. Let's have some fun
and entertainment in self-inflicted myopia.

All is well under the sun
until the next rendezvous
with Gaza indignant about its *baboukèt*,[4]
indignant about the Dominant Powers' hypocrisy
and about the logics that accommodates horrors
committed by friends and allies victorious in the war
launched in a huge prison of suffering souls
that Anderson Cooper could virtuously ignore,
the outrage is selective, you know,
because it's Gaza,
Gaza the rebel,
Gaza which refuses to die in silence.

(July 23rd, 2014)

Notes

1. AIPAC: American Israel Public Affairs Committee. Pro-Israeli lobby.
2. ISIS or ISIL: Islamic State of Iraq and the Levant, jihadist Sunnite group in Iraq.

3. CNN and MSNBC (respectively Cable News Network and Microsoft National Broadcasting Company, US cable televisions). MSNBC terminated their relation with Palestinian journalist Rula Jebreal because she criticized the pro-Israeli biases of the US media in a July 21st, 2014, live reporting. Nobody from the staff or the administration protested against this outrageous violation of journalistic freedom.

4. Baboukèt: Muzzle in Haitian.

The Thousand Sins of Piety and Love

Under the charm
and the spell of desire,
all seems to have meaning
suddenly—o eternal instant!

The mundanity of the passing time
at this juncture of destiny
has become a revelation to the living,
except that this time,
o mischievous time!
you are the prisoner of the spell of desire,
the one you call splendorous elation.

The reconfiguration of the senses
changes sins to virtues
celebrated as ethical conduct,
even the surest path to paradise.

Love as we know it on this land
is both a beautiful thing
and an ambush for many.
Still I love you,
you who embellish my road,
my road to nowhere
in the immensity of space.

My time with you is a treasure
of remembrance of time I did not waste;
it was the fulfillment of void.

Time walks its distance,
inexorably, regardless
of what people say,
independent of societal judgment.

One cannot trick time
although we ignore its appeal;
we may conquer space and its
surroundings, but not time,
the inescapable time.

Greed has invaded the space,
it marks the time of its venom
while the colonial mindset,
the domination of the space
and its living stock and sheep

pave the way to the reigning cynics
and the realists on grand scale.

All is possible on this Earth of ours
and the bridges that lead to nowhere
and the fabrication of fake monarchy
and the game of mirage control,
illusion that changed to disillusion.

I love the smell of human beings,
our embrace of the earthen treasure
deeply buried in the sub-oceanic world.

We share the same destiny
but you take too much of it;
let's rejoice together in our gains
and mourn together our losses,
the instant could be an eternity
for both you and the others.

You act as if you were
just like Rousseau had painted you,
you, the erector of fences, the one
that says: "This land is mine, only mine."
The rapacious eagle is looming
along the crossroads.

I admire the courage of the
fighting impetus for justice,
the millions who call for the abolition
of everything that hurts the child.

I admire you, you alone
in this long pursuit of time;
may your endurance to survive
calamities and bad luck in this life
be a bright light to all those who follow.

We must live as if we will
not be there the next day
like the death row inmate
out of stays and appeals.

I love the multiplicity
of life's beauty and variety.
the darkness after the sunset
as well as the sunny light
announcing the advent of dawn.

Our instant of encounter
is scripted in a corner of my memory
where the beatific, the stellar immensity
of space, the Cosmos, are intermingled,
blossoming in the multiple aspects of being.
We must make it a testimonial
to our passage on Earth
or a celebration of what really counts.

Nothing is new under the sun,
that much we know in this passing instant;
generations will come and go
so will the power to oppress and destroy
until a huge storm of hope takes the upper hand
and proclaims the emancipation of being
on this beautiful Earth of ours.

(July 2017)

The Tragic Waltz of the Wicked Eagles

Witnessing the Republican primaries of 2016 and the rise of Donald Trump

His talking points are not different
Of his incendiary rhetoric's lore
Simple categories of hate.
He wants to build a big wall, he says,
To keep Mexicans from returning home,
And the Cuban candidates sing along
Playing the most hawkish of the hawks.

The US is a country of damned souls searching solace
A continent away like all other wretched on Earth
Who leave their lands for a new world,
Or packed in the slave ship and forced to be here,
It's so familiar, you would say.
Still the front-runner's arrogance and luster
defies common sense and shows no restraint:
"Get them out! Get them out!", he says,
His Chant of war against valorous protesters
Whose loved ones were killed like rabbits
By racist cops with impenetrable blue khaki impunity
All bound by Omerta code version USA.
The protesters are our conscience's voice
Against madness and a meaningless jungle.

Many parents keep their children
From watching presidential debates
By fear of naughty contamination
From grown men prone to profanity
While the KKK and David Duke
Suddenly were unknown entity
Even when becoming mainstream as apple pie
Thanks to the ingenuity of the crude Don Dollar;
They are endowed with legitimacy
And once again the cross and the bank vault
And the buffoonery of the circus figurants
Win the day in media brouhaha
Golden boys with SS buttons is no sin.

Their performance is a tragedy
Under the guise of democracy
Replay of an unforgettable nightmare
In the daylight of reality.
Those seventeen men in pursuit
Of the highest office in the world

Like they say in conquerors' jargon
Are the lowest the mind could conceive
Amid this vast land of past glories.
This contest of Devil incarnates
Does not lend justice to a people
With such a multidimensional character
Even with different standards of decency.

The candidates' voices have called for exclusion
Of large numbers of the country's human beings
Playing who's-the-meanest of the town idiots
To appeal to the most hateful of the jerks,
To bring fear to the most excluded among us.
People's trepidation in the face of the rising bills
Conflicts with their unwillingness
To let their children get dummier
By men and women with closed minds
And huge ambitions and grandeur delusion.

The buffoon has played the jester on TV
And read a poem for children and cynics
Which speaks of an ungrateful snake
That kills his benefactor in earnest
After pleading for her to take him in,
This candidate equates traumatized Syrian migrants
Fleeing war horrors in search of a refuge
To the snake with murderous intent.
In the light of the history of this land
A land of torment, suffering and regret
Still under the spell of its genocidal past
And to have used its fragile truce
While awaken its basest of impulses
To serve your narrow and wicked interests,
Perhaps your family, migrants from Germany
Whose real name was Drumpt and not Trump
The more New York sounding of the two,
Perhaps you are the snake of the poem. Perhaps.

Large crowd of angry men and women
Claiming purity and ancestry and building walls
And scapegoat to their most profound anguishes,
That's what a Trump's rally looks like.
Beating on the most vulnerable among us
And claiming victory in a microphone
Is not America becoming a winner,
It's a bully preaching intimidation to a public

Zombified to the point of applauding joyfully
A CEO who is firing people from their work at will.
Large crowd of angry men and women
In jubilating ecstasy and holding the flag
And claiming the space as their sacred vital space.
Large and robust, military-looking men
Roughing up and beating protesters in a huge arena
Plus a charismatic leader leading on the charge
Against those he feels he can unashamedly dismiss
Without any cost to his power and standing
Are all familiar images we had seen before.

The discourse to banish and exclude the Other,
The venom on the visages of the huge crowd,
The targeting of minorities and all *alterities*
The raise fists and swear to the homeland
The debasing of human values and hope
Are all reminder of a horrible recent past.

They come today to demean the Muslims
They come today to demean the Mexicans
They come today to demean the Chinese
They come today to demean the Blacks
They come today to demean the Gays,
They will come tomorrow to demean your family;
Just like we are destroying the Earth that sustains us all
People have often brought their own hanging cord
Similarly of those who vote for these clowns.
The enablers like FOX News, CNN and MSNBC
Who give them a platform to spread their virus
Are all responsible for the broken jar.
Today they are ejecting protesters
And make fun of a woman's face and speech
And ridicule the gesture of the disabled,
Tomorrow they will target your own creed,
You are a fool if you fall for such a fallacy.

Still these grown men and women preaching
Stupidities to the well pre-programmed sheep
Are no aberrations nor even absurdities
Although their policy statements to a man
Are the weirdest in a world of unorthodox ideas.
They have not sprung from nowhere
Those angry enough to vote Trump
They're the recipient of many years
Of mistreatment by an unjust system,

Years of mixture of greed and media hype,
That blur what happens in people's real life
Just like the OJ fixation veiled the anti-crime law.

The Donald, parasite of money and privilege
Is also Father Bush blaming Willie Horton for USA's sins
While giving to real Wall Street mobsters a pass.
It's Bill Clinton making Sistah Souljah the sacrificial lamb
To reassure fearful, righteous and centrist Democrats
And Republican hardliners battling the black ghettos.
It's this same Clinton blaming so-called black Superpredators
And the Welfare Queens for disaster caused
By the Great Communicator and his rapacious minions,
The Robin Hoods for the rich and famous,
Heroic figure who claimed as his constituents of winners
The Jim Crow Democrats of the old and new South.
Still it is not what is absurd that hurts the most
But the methodically engineered scheme
To cheapen human beings for class-based profits.
It is not the clownish smirk that disturbs the most
But the final edict to banish from the perimeter
Of life's many splendors or the simple right to be
All those searching for the meaning of it all.

No, they have not sprung from nowhere, the candidates,
Wise are those young and not so young people who reject
The mirage of the false premises and promises,
I hold dear in my heart the courage to resist
The too easy road of human degradation,
The road to the darkness of our souls.

They are interchangeable in substance
And absence of substance in their talking points
They don't give it shit about the Republic
They are representation of just themselves
And feel disdainful toward the rest of us,
They are hilarious only to a point
For they're reaching to get hold of power,
Power to blow up our souls and our world.
They shall not pass! we must hell,
Oh, no, they shall not pass!

(April 2016)

The Elevation of the Better Barack
(A collage-reportage poem from Amiri Baraka's funeral)

His name is Amiri Baraka
and not simply Barack
he is not a Muslim
although he makes Muslim culture cool;
he sets forces on unsettling path
by shear poetic power and noise
and the ability to trigger
the rebellion of silence
and challenge the meanness of void.
Heavy police presence for the show
but the po-pos looked tired fighting the Brother
like Rochambeau saluting Capois-la-Mort's guts[1]
they surrendered to a higher drive for immortality
and laid out with Scottish bagpipes pomp
and the jubilation of the masses who don't believe
Amiri is dead anyway; they say he is still here with us
they say he is going nowhere
this is a stickup,
get out of here!
says Saul Williams with well-founded alarm.

They come from all over the United States
like birds returning to their original nest,
the blacks from the Black Arts Movement,
the reds from the Maoist Socialist branch
the Nation of Islam and its fruits
guarding the temple as treasure for posterity.
Malcolm's death was such a terrible deed
the enemy has set up the context
and the brother-kills-brother mindset.
Farrakhan has long reconciled the tribe
he defended the Shabazz from the vultures' grip;
he has sent his respect to Brother Ras and Sister
Amina Baraka for holding the flame;
Abdul Muhammad says, "Amiri stood on principle."
Tony Medina, a Brother from the hood blessed
with incendiary eloquence and streetwise pitch,
says Amiri Baraka is so bad he took Ariel Sharon with him
—the house went down in laughter; Brother Medina
says Amiri's tongue is a "language of Bopulicitous intent /
James Brown black Langston Hughes /
Mouth of Malcolm Baldwin eyes."

African drums like ancestral sacrifices
accompanied the rites in a jazz of words,
in a jazz of music, and maintained the tempo
Asha Bandele renders the meaning terse and dry,
in only a few words: "What a gift he gave us /
to those who have had so much taken."
Brother Askia Touré was there too,
Amiri's right hand youth and junior officer
of poet-led liberation army back in the day;
he is a survivor from the slaughter of time
and the CointelPro program that ravaged the hood,
he mourns his comrade with chants of glory
to elevate the soul, his words were for a family,
veteran of thousands of battles and sieges:
«Amiri Baraka», he yells, «présente !»

Brothers Everett Hoagland, Tony Van Der Meer,
and Tontongi were there too, along with Sisters
Soul Brown and Ashley Rose of Liberation Poetry creed;
they came down from the Boston cold to pay homage
to greatness bringing their Amazonian hearts
to warm those who stay the course.
Years before the big event, Hoagland wrote a poem
to extol the ancestral, rebellious lineage;
he salutes Baraka, saying like a prosecutor:
"you webbed the hood with barricades /
of barbed wire words / sharp as the amistad's cane knives…"
He says Amiri enlivened our dreams,
haunting the bourgeois' peace of mind.
The ushers carried the coffin up high
like a testament whose value they preserve
to the new generations of warriors incarnated
in children playing the trumpets rendering
a melody that cajoles and hurts
while enjoying the experience of a living ghost.
Danny Glover was there too
I envisioned him in the role of Toussaint,
he was now playing M.C. with Woodie King,
he says Amiri was his teacher, his inspiration;
Harlem, New York; Jackson, Mississippi;
Oakland, California; Chicago, Illinois;
Cleveland, Ohio; all lands of black torment
and black hope sent statements of comfort
to keep the fight alive.

In aging Newark Symphony Hall, the funeral unveiled
unflattering references to the darker chambers
of official business among a powerful governor
and his nemeses and associates doing openly
what they do behind Omerta's thick wall of silence
the imposing George Washington Bridge
being the ring for battles and child-like power plays.
Cornel West was there too his hair reaching to the sky
à la Albert Einstein and Don King,
"What a literary giant and kind revolutionary he was,"
says Brother West, elated.
"He dared to say Jesus was black,"
says another celebrant followed by a Chicago Brother
who says, reviving the music:
"We have just lost our John Coltrane
and our Langston Hughes,
Bush's successful negroes have supported ghosts."
How do you say goodbye to a god
—and not just welcome him?

Sonia Sanchez was there too
shorter than the speaker's lectern
but taller than us all even with pain-stricken face;
she says because of Brother Amiri's words
and struggle and teaching the world is now better;
she reads a loaded poem in cadence and all
that says everything one can say willingly
on death and dying and being dead and still resisting:
"The Cathedral of your death...
The Middle Passage of your death...
The blues of your death...
The Dialectic of your death...
The eyes of your death...
The teeth of your death...
The equal opportunity of your death...
The morning star of your death...
Can you repeat: Resist! Resist! Resist!
With tears and a lamenting voice
as if losing a battle in an uncertain war
a celebrant says with convictional tone:
"He was the most truly free black I ever met..."
"Yes, he was free!" agrees Brother Van Der Meer,
giving a metaphysical *wonga* strength to the words:
"He didn't let himself be blinded by greed
nor by vanity and celebretism."[2]

Brother Calvin X was there too,
earthbound from Oakland,
Baraka's companion in many street campaigns,
taken with gratitude and the solemnity of the occasion:
" Thank you for being a revolutionary, you show
that Black Arts and Black Power are one thing," he says.
Another celebrant, full of joy, agrees: "He gave us black people
a sense of power that would have been unthinkable before."

Michael Eric Dyson was there too, professorial ease
mixed with Black Baptist preacher theatrics
(some surmise he's too close to the liberal media charm),
he says, "History's language is music…
Amiri was a bridge between the streets
and the [presidential] cabinet…"
Alas, the cabinet is more black than power,
Amiri would have said,
but the Brother's point is well taken.
Amiri knew power is more the structure,
and more the ownership than the attitude
despite the sanctity of the deal
power is not the color of the cabinet
it is the ownership of the streets
it is the control of the Stock Market.

Maya Angelou sent her love and expressed her grief
for the loss of poetry and beauty,
while Savion Glover tap-danced as if to provoke
the coffin to break open and Amiri to join in,
defying destiny one more time.
Lawrence Hamm says, "He was the spirit of revolution."
Ras Baraka is the family's new lion,
the dauphin that becomes the reigning king, the Ras;
he has the tongue and the daring stand, the temerity
to tell truth to power, his eulogy was as much an appeal
to clean up the mess as a reflection on a loved and loving dad;
it was a celebration as well as a long lament for lost time,
it was music, poetry, chant of distress, exhortation
to challenge fate, to resist systemic malfeasance:
"My father titled his last book Razor because he wants
to cut some people before he gets out of here," he says.
Through the son's voice and demeanor,
through the flow of the words,
through the huge collective embrace, and warmth
emitted by the jubilant crowd, Ras' words reinforced

what Sister Souljah said:
"I thought Ras's family was rich," she says,
"because he had a father I thought he was rich
because he had a family that talked to each other,

I thought he was rich
because the family was engaged in the community."
Cast in a river of words that flew unhindered,
forming unity of destiny, Ras' eulogy, poignant,
reaffirmed the essence of existing and being,
being Amiri Baraka
the rebel that destroyed silence.

Brother Amiri Baraka's passing
as that just weeks before of Nelson Mandela,
warriors for the elevation of the Earth's wretched
only pass the torch to younger hands
newer blood for the ancestors' renewal.

When I was tormented in exile's loneliness
his words represented the poet's refusal
to bow to artificiality made holy reality;
he was the poet that seeks total freedom
amid the misery of the instant even at the price
of danger one faces in following one's conscience.
Yes, the world is a better place because of Baraka,
despite continuing horrors and oppression.

(January 2014)

Notes

1. Capois-la-Mort is the nickname of Haitian officer François Capois who, during the last battle for Haiti independence on November 18, 1803, impressed so much French general Viscount of Rochambeau that he halted the fight to give military salute to Capois's bravura.
2. Wonga: Vodou curse in Haitian Creole.

From the left: **Tontongi, Edwidge Danticat, Paul Laraque and Patrick Sylvain at Laraque's house in Queens**, NY in 2002.

It's New York

The parade of the brave
the joyful constellation
of colors, light, laughter,
the rainbow of undesirables
claiming their right to the place;
it's their day of glory
it's their day of pride.

It's New York
the so-called Big Apple
for heartless billionaires
bound by no constraint
and big, unrelenting stress
for everyone in-between.

It's New York
the fearless amazon
who goes it alone
when she must

and should.

It's New York
the depraved of Gomorrah
who's opened it's long
and soaring shores
to all Earth's wretched
fleeing horrors perpetrated
in the name of the Fatherland
and in the name of God and his
self-proclaimed representatives
while some others have claimed it
as theirs and nobody else.
It's New York
where the Biblical Jonah
after weeks of induced homelessness
is resuscitated on 31st Street
in the "Brothers Size" play[1]
resurfaced in a super-off Broadway joint
enough for the evangelicals to renew
their oath to Trump and his minions.
It's New York
where I first witnessed the distortion
of love and the human body
and the depravity of freedom
along the 42nd Street and other
parts where the sweat-shops of infamy
held shop amid distress and tears
while many dreams died in despair.
It's New York
where it seemed to take ages to find
the police crossing exit along the 5th Avenue
where the parade went along
amid boisterous, carnival-like enthuse
and great artistic rendering.

It's New York
where Jill and I visited with
Maura, Arthur and Kathy
along the hill of the Morningside Park,
talking about questions of our time
and other pleasantries and reminiscences.
We later were joined after a promenade
on the sunny streets of New York
by Kenji, Didi, Naomi, Davy and Jonah,

all savoring together a lavish meal
made of Haitian and Thai cuisines;
it's New York
you now know.
It's New York
on an end of June
the heat immersing
in the sensual skin of the people
beautiful people of this part of the Earth.

It's New York, my friend,
and whatever the fuck you feel
you're entitled to the prison
of your inner soul and lore;
you're also entitled, remember, to the conquest of infinity.

It's New York
where many of my loves were born
and buried in somber cemeteries;
New York where my tears flew
along the river of blood,
and where my gaze refused to blur.

It's New York
where amid drama and sadness
our species rendezvous
for the quest of freedom.

It's New York
on this day when virtue and sin
are no longer on opposite sides,
a day of glory and pride

Note

1. My son Jonah performed in the play "Brothers Size" at the Imperial Loft Theater in Manhattan, New York, on June 2017.

What Resilience Ain't[1]

Shouldn't be resignation
nor Idontgiveitdamness
of the soul and the mind;
it shouldn't be devotion
to the shallowest of ideas
of those connected to mundanity
and to the crass impulse of the flesh
inhibiting the sound judgment
even of the wisest of the sages.

It shouldn't be the ditching
to survival's black hole
of your most sacred values
only to delay for one day
the inevitability of what should be.

It shouldn't be masochism
of self-hated victims of oppression
giving up the struggle for freedom
to secure a less unpredictable fate.

It should not be delegation
to the most idiotic among us
or to Wall Street's greediest ethos
of our right to a dignified life.

It shouldn't be accommodation
to nature's maddening onslaught hidden
under the guise of faith, law and order
while the culprit is closer to home.

It shouldn't be accepting intolerance
and inequality and an unjust order
and what you're told since childhood
as being reality and cosmic destiny.

It shouldn't be endurance and only that
but rather patience joined with conscience;
rather the other side of the Universe
the unknown multitude lost in banality
and in the indifference of absence.

Rather the engagement in the Absurd
than the myopia of the perception;
rather the feeling of the pain
and the glory of the last stand
than the pathetic robot's state.

Rather the phoenix's metamorphosis
than the unending torpor-like routine
rather the resistance to *finitude*
than the boredom of the same-old-thing.

It shouldn't be habituation
to the conditioning of the senses
nor the appeasement of the libido
by the Behavior Control Department.

Resilience should not be atonement
nor penitence for imaginary sins;
it's the re-hurrah of the last hurrah
it's the zombie vengefully tasting salt
despite the master's objection.[2]

It's the wretched conquering the Temple
it's the beauty of the poetic word
the elegance of the liberated zest
the magic of the love song
the everlasting conquest of the beast
by the simple majesty of art and folly.

(April 2012)

Notes

1. This poem was written especially for the Spring 2012 issue of Auscultation, a journal published by the staff of Cambridge Health Alliance whose 2012 issue was devoted to Resilience. The journal published a shorter version but the whole poem was read by the author at the release gala on June first, 2012, at Cambridge Hospital.
2. In Haitian mythology a zombie will regain consciousness if he/she tastes salt.

Why Did Dunkin' Donut Empty the Place of Undesirable People?

The place is known by everyone
in this Central Square of ours
as the Donut Place
painted in white and pink.

A place open to all
where street people
homeless people
people in between
people who are escaping work
people who don't want to think
people who want to break the day
came for coffee and a space to relax.

I valued the pleasure
of mingling with people
who have other concerns than mine.

The Donut Place
was the only social space for many

who couldn't afford to spend
more than a single minute
in any given place
in this rather spacious
and flourishing square.

The Donut Place
had a certain funkiness
which gave it an air of authenticity
with its multiple connections
of lives in Central Square
with its human suffering at plain view
the mixture of rich university kids
and nouveau middle class residents
(as we say of nouveau rich and all)
and intolerant new comers
with clout and attitude,
the old Cambridge who still resists
along with the uprooted Cantabrigians
who still endear it in their hearts,
they all participate in its splendors
and also its chagrin
its somnolence in *developers'* mantra
and the take-over by the corporations.

The Donut Place
didn't mean much to me
but for others it was
their urban home and headquarters
the place where lost souls
in the light of an instant
would find a little connivance
with reality and its negation
also with its dead-ends
and possibilities.

After months of absence
one day I returned
innocent and happy
to the Donut Place
and saw with utmost bewilderment
three long, round tables
and not a single seat around
in the Donut Place of our hearts.

I saw there
an empty space
devoid of humans.

I tried to imagine
the motivating ideals
of the Dunkin' Donut's birth
in this Quincy town of Boston
then I realized I couldn't know,
to each time its madness.
(Most of the above-mentioned visitors are no longer welcome
to the Donut Place. That's our time's madness…)

(March 30th, 2019)

Glory on 17th October

Dedicated to the Haitian demonstrators fighting against government corruption

I tip my hat to you,
brave soldiers of the streets
longtime banished
to life's anguish
away in life's absence
in the silence of horror,
outside the compass
of our consciousness.
I still cherish that day
on a sunny October 17th
along tumultuously stoic
Port-au-Prince in revolt
on the day of the Emperor's
demise when you resurrected
his ideals for freedom
toward infinite horizons.
I joined with you that day
elated in solidarity
with your noble cause
and with those who died
at the hands of their tormentors
May your cries and strife
for a better world find echo
in the everyday pursuit of beauty.

From the left: **Charlot Lucien, Marie Evangéline Roussel, Jill Netchinsky & Tontongi at the Boston Poetry Festival reading at the Boston Public Library** in 2024.

From the left: **Jonah Toussaint, Jill Netchinsky & Tontongi at a wedding in Plymouth**, MA, in July 2023.

From the left: **Everett Hoagland, Soul Brown & Tontongi** at a poetry reading in Cambridge, Massachusetts in 2015.

Where the Square Wanderer Sleeps

He walks in a quiet, smooth and slow pace

Along the busty square in meditative trance;
Even his panhandling conveys some elegance
A sort of misplaced contempt for money and vanity.

His sense of fashion defies all standards and tastes:
Black trash bags hanging around his waistline like

a chef's apron that reaches down the ankle expressing
No particular inkling other than a unique flair.

He sleeps with a bundle of multilayered inventive
And handy covers which still leave one to wonder

How does he survive the diabolic New England

Winter snow storm with such frailty means of endurance?

The slow traffic on Massachusetts Avenue
Is of no interest to him being in his own universe;
His all living is unsafe but that's not a concern
As are not the hazards threatening his well-being.

What is his story, I asked myself many a time
When seeing him so disengaged, while his stares
Conveyed a deep contemplation of the Unknown,
A hubris of grandeur even when facing horrors.

Living in such indifference and social emptiness
The wanderer probably needs either a Bill Gates with

A heart or the Soviet turmoil to blow up the all mess.
How the hell is he able to survive in such empty hole?

How does one live amid a crowd of consuming zombies?
Why couldn't Harvard, MIT, Cambridge and Lesly colleges
Build a most wonderful mansion along the Charles River
On the Memorial Drive where the homeless can come…

…And hang out and take a shower even be provided with
Counseling and learning a new trade? Why not having
A new life in between, a new sense of the self and the world?
Why don't the real-state moguls who've sucked so much this…

…Land lend a hand in making of this place a welcoming oasis?
The Square wanderer doesn't even ask for that much, being
In his own world, admiring the wonders of the city life,

just Going around, wandering and wondering 'til the night comes.

(December 2019)

Haiti Is Not What You Say, Mr. Tèt-Mato[1]

Haiti is the island nation born
from the cross-Atlantic blood
of people sold to the Traders.

Haiti actualizes the meaning
of both being and living
and has invented a new path
to freedom and a new way
to detect its perversion
even in the dark of the night.

Haitians shed blood for the United States
on the battlefield of Savannah
these valorous fighters held the lines
against British onslaught
to save the birth of the Republic
and help this nation into being.

Haiti is the country that stood
to her own peril and harm
against almighty France,
Spain and England
over the inalienability of being.

Haiti is the foundation of our modernity,
Haiti is the unsung mother of Latin America;
Haiti is where Francisco de Miranda and Simón Bolívar
came to acquire the fervor of brotherhood
and resources to liberate their lands.

Haiti has made hers, heroic and brave
countless other countries' causes
for human freedom and independence,
the most Hellenic nation of Greece among them.

Haiti is not what you say, Mr. Tèt-Mato;
Haiti is the country of the once enslaved
who dared to resist oppression
and whose bravura in defeating Napoleon's forces
compelled him to sell the Louisiana territories,
doubling the size of US possessions of the time;
a favor that is now honored with insults.

Haiti is the land of the arts
where writers, poets, storytellers,
musicians, painters, sculptors wrought
the infinitesimal inner souls of our Universe.

Haiti is among the richest countries in the world
by measure of intellectual and philosophical
achievement of her people's genius
and for the beauty of this mountainous land
despite the human-made pollution aided and abetted
by U.S. support of corrupt dictators.

Haiti is not what you say, Mr. Tèt-Mato;
Haiti has sent to North America's shores
thousands of doctors, researchers, intellectuals
and teachers who instill values
that enliven and enrich the children's fortitude;
some of her migrants scrub your floors
and take care of your sick and feeble;
Haiti has been good to the United States.

Haiti is the country forced to pay
in billions of French francs
and National City Bank bonds
for having won her freedom;
the people's sweat was made
to sweeten many a Western high life
while the first Black republic
languished in impoverishing debt.

This descent into the abyss of darkness,
the degrading remarks that demean
hurt like a sword that penetrates the heart;
we shall not mince words; we shall see it plain,
naked in its nature, representing a deeper ill,
a more widely-shared sentiment.

The menace of hate coming from the voice
of the highest symbol of U.S. power
today targets the Haitians
today targets the Africans
today targets the Muslims
today targets the Mexicans
today targets the Salvadorans
today targets the Iranians
today targets the Palestinians
is the same that targeted the Jews,
the Socialists, the Communists,
the Gypsies, the Homosexuals.
the Jehovah's Witnesses, the mentally
and physically handicapped,

and we know what happened then.
The menace will tomorrow target you
and all people who don't look Norwegian...[2]

O Africa! Cradle of the civilization
of men and women inventing humanity!
O Africa! The land of the Mandé Charter
where human rights were first made sacred
on a day in thirteenth-century Mali,
today demeaned by a knuckle-head!

The immigrants come to the land of immigrants
where Christian pilgrims, vagabonds, ex-cons,
persecuted of all stripes come to find refuge;
the land where defeated Ottoman subjects,
and pre-Nazi German nationals
came to become rich,
some leaving behind the values
of common human bonds;
the land where Jews, Christians, Muslims,
Buddhists, Taoists, Vodouists,
Irish, Japanese, Somalians,
and all kinds of disadvantaged
come to find their peace
although not always in welcoming fuss.

You have no right to deny others
that which serves your family well
and makes you a successful,
arrogant nouveau riche;
you have no right, however large
your ill-acquired fortune may be,
to debase whole continents of diverse nations;
you are a disgrace to mankind.

What we are seeing today
and experiencing in real time
is no longer an innocent joke
when real men, women, and children
are paying the heaviest price.
We must take to the streets
the fight for human integrity,
if we want to hold on to our dreams;
the tragic comedy already lasts too long.

A lone white supremacist at the White House
I would dismiss without much ado, but a system

that lets a lunatic destroy its ideals, my friend,
this is the problem we all should condemn.

I hold the whole system of government,
endowed to foster harmony and well-being
and to guide our children to higher pursuit,
responsible for letting this barbarian into the gate.
It's time to stop the power of greed
and the corruption of our institutions!

The world will never forget
this affront to human decency,
nor will the masses of the United States
forgive endurance of such shame.

Haiti is not what you say;
Your Haiti is a reflection
of your twisted phantasms;
our Haiti is the guardian of our light
that which makes us all human;
your Haiti is a black hole
ours is a Deleuzian structure
a place where many dimensions join
in the pursuit of elevation
a place where many splendors coalesce.[3]

(Boston, January 13th, 2018)

Notes

1. This poem was written in response to Donald Trump's insults in calling Haiti and the whole continent of Africa "shithole countries." The term «Tèt-Mato» means "Hammer-Head" in Haitian Creole and generally refers to a dabbler, a crude person.
2. In allusion to Donald Trump's remark that only people from countries like Norway should be allowed to immigrate to the United States.
3. This poem was also published in the trilingual anthology, *This Land, My Beloved* (2024).

Second Period Poetics

Bar thought and all

Mawonnaj (Marooning)

We Haitian are good
in the game of mawonnaj
emulating and beating stress
in our daily lives.

We marooning in Heaven
just as in Hell if it should be;
we marooning like our ancestors
did in times of challenge;
we marooning to stay true
to our most inner feeling
for this life imposed on us
and of which we're making
an ideal and a dream.

March 31st, 2017

Just like it has been so far
for Trump this month is hell
for me and surely for others.
Hell is too much, I agree,
of a term to use here,
maybe a simpler, less
of a pompous word
or existential word
would do, I would think.
The time asks us to care
about building barricades
against fascism and hate.
200 civilians in Musil
dead in a strike.
And not much was said about it.
Let's spell it: say 200 lives
lost in a single strike
have no meaning
in life's realm
of troubling events.

The idea that crosses my mind
in this instant of confusion is:
why can't we invent
a new way of being together
and live contingence?

April 1st, 2011

I met many daughters
I don't have nor conceive
—and she is one of them,
I will not tell her so.
I want her to believe
women are not only body
nor desire's satisfaction target,
but also a soul that embodies
the land lost in the passage
to the reign of greed.

April 1st, 2017 (continued)

She surprises the place
a popular bar right in the Square
she writes by vocation
I do the same, I told her,
but she works too much
for the bar and not enough
for her own good which is writing
whatever inspiration comes to mind.

I told her it should be a trade-off:
me giving you my time for your company,
you giving money for my own company
and enough time to do both.

She said, with a long smile
on her face radiating:
"I'll write that down."

How Do You Tell the End?

How do you tell
if tomorrow the smile will dry
like a summer heat wave's spell?

How do you tell him
this season might be his last
and that the Square's pigeons
will no longer enjoy his crumbs?

How do you tell him
his God is ready to let him
go to his ultimate fateful road
which his custom-made destiny
had preconceived for him?
How do you tell him
his doctor thinks his chance
is as small as a calendar year
and that over it is a stretch?
How do you tell a man
Mother Earth will reject
his living equal right among us
and that the end is near?
How do you tell him
that's not the eternity that counts
but the quality of the moment
the immaterial joy of the fugitive instant
that transcends the *finitude* of the body?

From the left: **Tontongi, Stona Fitch and Madison Smartt Bell** at a reading in Concord, Massachusetts, in 2012.

Orwellian Three-Month Time

Only three months into Neo-Nero's apotheoses
many people are already tired of him
and of his antics and scandalous
compromise with money and bad taste.
Only three months after Don Dollar's
rise to power the country is petrified
in its sudden awakening in Orwellian
fantasies and worries
still the resistance is stronger
than even pre-1776
one hopes.

(March 2017)

Collective Scream of Joy

Everyone suddenly was screaming
with yell of enjoyment,
two teams of basketball players
with dreadful and deadly determination
were fighting it under the excitement
of the crowd 'till the very end.

A collective scream of joy
had defeated a complaint of distress.
Why has sport taken after the symbolisms of war
and not after our collaborative togetherness?

A Drink From a Beautiful Stranger

I went to this neighborhood bar
right in the middle of Union Square
on a pre-Spring cool night.
Then a young, punky-looking
but beautiful lady bartender
managerial style
or palace governess like
served me a cold,
good beer;
I asked her how much?
She just said: "It's on me."
"She looks beautiful and human, "I thought,
"She's paid her passage to greatness
by giving a Black man a free drink
in the Trump's era," I concluded in thought.

(Naturally, ultra-right racism is pervading the moment, we must
emphasize the relevance of meaning. I still don't know why
she gave me the drink, still the poetics of the gesture remains
to this day an undetermined and unexplained causality.

A Drink From a Beautiful Stranger (continued)

At the closing time in the bar,
I went back to the young, attractive bartender,
her gaze questioning my intent.
I told her with a voice that conveyed
both tenderness and the quest for ideals
and high dreams: "Thank you for the drink
I was thinking of leaving you a tip,
I decided instead to come to shake your hand
and show my gratitude in person."
She answered, "Thank you to you too,"
with a brilliant light crossing her face.

Deconstructing Our Mental State

The day started
in a slowly instilled pain
by the news early on
that we've been evicted.
Life is so ironic and vile
a moron has the White House
and the Manhattan Trump Tower
while a Yale PH.D. and rebel poet
are looking for an apartment,
the muse and the Academy
there's no place for them
in the USA of today
that's deconstruction
of our mental state.*

> *Play of words of Trump's former adviser Steve Bannon who vowed to "deconstruct the administrative state."

Bad News

Fake news
selected news
are two sides
of the same aim
Wall Street and Main Street
red states and blue states
making claims of the land.
Exclusion of the Other
and all other others
that don't make claim
—or do they?—
of our USA.

Get Rid of Your Hang Up

If you're undocumented
that doesn't make you "illegal".
Christopher Columbus was undocumented
so were the first settlers in this vast
last land of hope not yet named the USA.
Let's stop the non-sense,
tell yourself you probably resent your "immigrant" neighbor
for not being caught up
in your psycho-hang-ups.

It's Not the Race, Nor the Color, Idiot

It's not the race
nor the color, idiot;
it's the conditioning of the soul;
it's the management of emotions
to profitable input and gain.
It's not the race
nor the color, idiot,
it's you and others refusing to resist
and conceding victory to those
lost in their selfish selfie self.

We are pained by other's decisions and whims and madness, but we're not responsible for their occurrence, nor their possibility. We are affected by others' *un-exposition* to multiple dimensions of the coin, still we can tell them that dreaming is okay. The human soul is made of both matter, and the many contingencies that happen in survival—and spirit, in the sense of what Sartre calls the ability to transcend the ego, the unattached self.

Which One of the Oligarchs?

"The oligarchs," he said
sitting next to me in the bar…
Which ones? I wondered,
how do they coexist
with the homeless man
in the street corner,
and the teenage mother
on WIC support?

I saw earlier tonight an episode of "Believer" on CNN talking about Haitian Vodou and all. It gave me a feeling of déjà vu, like re-seeing Reverend Pat Robertson saying his moronic thing about Haiti's contracting a pact with Satan for having liberated itself from colonization and slavery. And for which the earthquake was pay-back. That's a rubbish predicate people are still saying in the Internet era of this 21st century.

As Devoted a Woman Could Be

She is full of life
a beautiful smile on her face
she radiates of splendor
and has a big you know what
as devoted a woman could be
on saint Patrick's Day.

No Reversing Role

She looks like the daughter
I would have had
If I were a white man.
I didn't dare telling her so.
White women just don't imagine
black men as their father, I thought.
The reverse, therefore, doesn't apply.
I didn't tell either
of the other thought she inspired…

How would a life without the sound of music feel like? "No worse," one would say, still the song from the radio smoothed my soul and alleviated the feeling of dependency to other's whim and caprices and stupidities that have crossed my *entendement*. Total freedom of being and breathing should be of easy reach to humans and animals in all geographical areas. So should music.

Daring Little Bug

(A Surrealist poem)

The other idiot sitting in the next chair
is more curious than a rabbit under the spotlight of the half-lighted bar,
somber with lonely men, and a few women faking happiness.

That was a harsh condemnation,
I concurred, of a man I know
only for his nosy, staring gaze,
I was also not in the mood
to be disturbed by non-sense

I saw a little bug running along
the bar's drink-preparing section,
this small counter where a panoply
of draught, brand-name beers formed
a column of their own, like the juices'
and I wondered whether the little bug
would not end up in my drink.
I changed the subject, seeing the trap
of confining my soul in bug's mind.
And intent.

The next moment improved by the appearance of a beautiful
half-Asian and half-anything woman
in this world of lonely men and the
atmosphere changed. But the place
was still the same, the men continued
to watch games scattered in all three
tv screens. At this point of the night
the new half-Asian and half-anything woman
had lost all interest in the place, immersing
herself in her Apple smartphone,
a more reliable company.
By now the bug was gone.

What About If We Talked?

In the bar across town
from Cambridge to Boston
just across the bridge good sense
would preferably call MIT Bridge
that people here call Harvard Bridge
although Harvard is one mile away
because when it was first built
MIT and its Roman columns
were not even there, being
farther down in rebellious Boston.

I love the people who work there.
We never exchanged a word for a long time,
but then one night all was said
in candid chats, just talking for the fun of it.
We engaged everyone in the conversation
on Being and Being there.
The language of the Other,
the wall that separates us all.
I told them about my friend in
a small town near Reims in France
with whom I was doing the *vendanges*
in the long lines of grape vines
who didn't steal anything from my suitcase
while he emptied everyone's else.
A very intelligent woman said,
as if to make me grasp other possibilities:
"What about if your friend was playing
a game to just unsettle you?"

The question was so non-linear
I thought she was tending me a trap.

P.S.

I misplaced the ending stanza of my poem on God knows what, I replace it, hereby, by this statement of faith and poetic license:
We are all greedy
when the greenback flows
and rent-control dismissal brings prosperity and peace of mind, out the strangers and trouble-makers,
welcome peaceful yuppies,
rich kids making millions on the side.
The neighborhood is now saved
boredom we can stand.

In a way I enjoy as self-flagellation
the unsettling meanness of Trump
and the US's conservative right
who is free-riding with his tweets.

"Killing Me Softly With His Song"

At this after-hour bar in Cambridge,
precisely on Cambridge Street, I heard
this song "Killing me softly with his song"
by the lovely, captivating Roberta Flack.
I remember my teenage years in Carrefour,
a suburb turned shantytown in Port-au-Prince
where happiness, fear of tonton-macoutes,
bleak future of a whole generation
couldn't keep away thought of elevation,
conquest of the world, love and all.
Beauty of youth. Beauty in Hell.

If He Stays He's Staying For Life*

If he stays one more month
the next will bring his fall,
if he stays two more months
the next will bring his fall,
if he stays one more year
the next will bring the fall day,
if he stays two more years
the Midterm may change the game,
if he stays after that
he can stay for four years.

If he stays until four years
he would be reelected
if he stays over four years
after being reelected
by the same rigged voting
they will make him the
life-long king of the republic.

If he stays after being made
the life-long king of the republic
no one will ever look
oneself in the mirror again,
and the United States
will never be the same.

Having been able to stay
for any length of time at WH Inn,
it's a sign that perhaps we have fooled ourselves
and everybody else.

> *This quasi-premonitory poem was written during the first year of the Trump administration (2017), that is three years before coup attempt of January 6, 2021.

Never Provoke a Madman

You don't incite a madman
to react to bad things that happen,
there could be a price to pay
if you criticize his inaction
and make him feel like a wimp.

While tyrants respect force
a madman could care less
even much less when his fate

is still in flux in his entanglement

with Russian spies, and offshore banks

and election hackers from the same shore
that are haunting him in his sleep.

While you should have been grateful
that he ignored North Korea's ballistic
test and Syria's use of saran gas
against its foes while the tyrant's own
Air force just a couple of weeks prior
had killed two hundred civilians;
and you seem now to want him
to blow up things as kid do with Nintendo;
you must make up your mind,
you can't expect sensational ratings
and also peace of mind in paradise;
you can't blow up Mohamed's village

in Mosul and have a wonderful
and peaceful time in Time Square.

You can't expect him to be a buffoon
when you also make him the head

of the offensive against Obamacare

while T-Party red-necks are applauding;
you can't expect him to be a fuck head
and still ask him to save your majority.

You can't ask a moron or a pretender
to be king and complain he is not up
to the task; you can't ask the Donald
to perform and satisfy your phantasms
and thrills and condemn him for being
true to himself and whatever else he does.

Gasoline and Matches
Mixing Kim Jong-Un and Donald Trump
in a problematic of war and peace

is like mixing gasoline and matches.

Yesterday was the happening
of a Great North Korea Parade,
Missiles, ICBM and all exposed[1]
for the republic people to rejoice on.
The streets were clean and polished,
perfect like only law and order can do.

Today Kim Jong-un's missile launch
was reported to have failed in medias

all over the world as relief, but his failed
launch called the bluff of Trump

and High Command who seems

to have taken control in quiet mode.[2]

Today, thousands all over the USA
and aboard go to the streets to demand
change of priority from the government
and respect for all immigrants and their
rights to be in the land of the free
and that no human being be killed

like rabbit in their names
and that peace be the only option.

(April 15, 2017)

Notes

1. ICBM: Intercontinental Ballistic Missile.
2. In allusion to US Secretary of State General Alexander Haig who declared "I am in control," the day of the assassination attempt on Donald Reagan on March 30, 1981, even though cabinet secretaries are in 4th position in the line of succession.

Destiny and Living

Destiny tests human resolve
and resilience and capacity
to endure serial adversities
in the name of living
living life's charge of stress,
and pleasure in little things.

We create our own Absolute
and cultivate our own will to explore
the many roads leading to hope.
We can also join with each other
to invent new ways of being.
Being in here and now, being
in solidarity with the underdogs,
those not born with silver spoons
in their mouths and asses.

The Bar as Oasis

The bar provides
an oasis of détente
from Trump and Russian news;
the happy beautiful faces
all around the counter
and surrounding tables;
the flow of booze
and food on demand
added all pleasant vibes
to the night and my mood.
"Life still has meaning," I thought,
"Life is good," as JDJ likes to say,*
life is good indeed
in spite of the venom called Trump,
April Fool of the year.

(April 1st, 2018)

* JDJ is the initials of my friend, the poet Jean-Dany Joachim

Thanks God That the Dance of Death Was Canceled

Sure enough our juvenile president
sent over an armada a few days
after his threat of mayhem and malfeasance
to his North Korean counterpart,
this would be the Dance of Death
between two crazies who deservedly
belong to the protective wall of an asylum.

You don't elect a madman
and expect him to be normal;
you don't elect a perverted man
and expect him to make you proud;
you don't sleep with the Devil
while you wish to reach for goodness.

How Do You Change a Bad Narrative?

Sandwiched between three monsters

He threw 59 tomahawk missiles
on a deserted Syrian air field
killing a few army men
supposedly bad hombre
who two days earlier
tossed chemical bombs
on civilian innocent people
and beautiful children to whom
that he had not too long ago
refused refuge on his land.

As expected in hawkish land
McCain and Graham applauding
the advent of war and coming glory
the colonial and imperial mindset
take over these righteous souls,
Reason has become immaterial
while the Master of illusion
and disorientation leads the way.

Dangerous is the man who has so much
to lose and must fight for his brand,
killing a few more Syrians after all,
doesn't a difference make if we can get the Russians
after initial expression of repulsion
to go along in tactical cordiality,
God bless the USA.

The whole thing could be a comedy
if real people didn't pay for it,
we all know what took place
in the dark of the night
misogynous adrenaline in action
billions of greenbacks in the balance
great powers deconflicting in tacit recognition
of share of influences and respective
prerogatives on a desert of suffering.
It's a good way to change the narrative
on the treasonous deeds to subvert
the Republic's democratic ideals
in the service of the motherland.
Dangerous is the man we so trust
to save us and who himself is mad as hell!

Please, just ask him one last question
to test the wisdom of his fake optics:
Would you, Mister President, let
the beautiful Syrian children come
to your land for refuge?
A simple question, won't you say?
Dangerous is the man who can send
submarine saboteurs on the coast
to play war games with his counterpart
on this sad day of madness of un-grown
men armed with nuclear arms and all.
It's the mess we're in, my friends,
at this moment of our time.
How do you change a bad narrative?
You threw 59 tomahawk missiles
on an isolated airfield in Syria
and send submarine saboteurs on the coast,
write a crazy tweet in the middle of the night,
say you gonna cozy up to Bibi
and ban Iran from the Persian Golf;
tell the press you gonna bomb China,
and nobody will have a chance
to question neither your past dealing
with the Russians and all
nor the long legacy of corruption
and the double hitting on the little man
will ever see the light of day.

(April 2017)

A Strange Time For a Strange Country

The news was about investigation of Russian intelligence's involvement with Donald Trump's campaign operatives to subvert the 2016 presidential election

That was the news
and the operating principle
to go to the bottom of it
and find culprits and enablers
twenty-four hours around
talking about Nunes' complicity*
in obstructing justice and manipulating
the media brouhaha until
conventional Ethics laid him a trap
that he couldn't game anymore.

It would take an anti-mafia overhaul
to make this comedy a past reality,
but it will remain as it is, my friend,
until we throw the bum out.

It's your legacy, you, the corporate media
who make everything stop suddenly
and talk non-stop about all-thing Trump
over and over around the clock
and eclipsing seventeen other candidates
and playing the Trumpian game;
it's your legacy, you know,
you the so-called free press.

> *Devin Nunes, former congressman, chair of the House Intelligence Committee from 2015 to 2019.

What Does Really Count?

What does really count?
Is it your swindle of land and resources

of Mother Earth for your personal use
and abuse and neglect?

Tell me, what does really count?
Is it your greed and caprices
or the cry of the malnourished child
or the emptiness of homelessness?

What does really count?
Is it the Earth losing her protective
shield due to rapacious foraging?

What does really count?
Is it the instant or the eternity?
Is it the family trying to live a normal life
or you destroying it with your policies
or a lovely walk on the sunny beach?
Is it what you think or what you feel?

[The young man who is serving us drinks
in this after-hour bar near my son's former
school in East Cambridge, now unaffordable
ike the rest of the city of our heart,
understands it's the caring that counts,
the place's character, it's feel of human vibes.
The rest is the flippancy of fake reality.]

Revelation

Marie Lagone suddenly comes to me
in Harvard Square this afternoon of a hot summer;
she came to me all black
corsage black and skirt black
and a black hat that makes her
look like Papa Gede on November 1st.
She mumbled a few words
that seemed outside apprehension.
Marie Lagone was beautiful
before she was gone to the darkness;
I ask her "Why are you in all black ?",
she says "I'm enjoying the transformation
to a different state of being."
Marie Lagone was never gone
she just changed her universe.

Marie Lagone is our Goddess
put under the spell of madness,
on her Gede appearance in the Square
she exhibited the sexiness of time passed
when with Rodney on her side
she conquered Cambridge
and all her beauty,
the conscience of her community
she was, steadfast in her fight
for the right of us all to be.

He Is as Apple Pie as US-America

He is as apple pie as US-America
from your church looking asshole
from asshole looking churchy
from the slicing of Manhattan
from greedy landlord to the Oval office,
from the alienated lumpen masses
who dream and long muse
of a new Eldorado on the Hudson.

He is yours, the Donald,
don't pretend to deny
your flirtation
nor your affiliation;
he is yours, the Donald,
your Avida Dollars*
in twenty-first century USA.

> *Avida Dollars, anagram of Salvador Dalí's given to him by the Surrealists because of his greed.

Third Period Poetics

Poems of hope and resilience in the times of Covid-19

Carefree Geese on the Charles River

Amid the pandemic's haughty
And haunting specter, I seek
The company of the birds
On sunny Memorial Drive;
Few souls have ventured about
On this early Spring afternoon,
Still the geese, in boisterous
Manner, have sung back to me.

For the first time I feel ashamed
Of liking them so much;
But the passing instant
Has reaffirmed life's meaning.

(Cambridge, Massachusetts, April 3, 2020)

The Lifeline Power of a Smile

Dedicated to the healthcare workers on the front lines

The Big Doom Scourge with
Pompous name of COVID-19
Has mimicked the quiet, sneaky
Way of a vengeful rodent mixed
With the indifferent cold-bloodedness
Of a deceitful purveyor of mass hysteria,
Sowing fear, grief, and destruction
Along with the atrophy of city life.
It has come all of a sudden
This remaking of vital fusion
Of energy and elation
Seeming to redirect exchanges
Between Eros and Thanatos;
The reimagination of the body
Seen from now on as an alterity
Of joyful attraction and dreadful
Disinterest of an invisible curse.
Yet even when egocentric impulses
Of self-preservation and wellbeing
Become the rigid law of the land,
Even in the worried and hurried pace
Of passer-by strangers honoring
The 6-feet protocol of social distancing,
Sometimes filtered a furtive smile
Radiating the delight of the human spirit.

Even surrounded by machines and tubes
Amid the cleanliness of disinfected
White rooms, the loneliness of isolation,
Arises the health provider's calming touch
Armed with a subtle, tender smile.
In this ultimate moment for the afflicted
Even for the dying on their way out
Humanity has reaffirmed its essence,
The gift of simple pleasure of being,
Rebirth from the cavalry of desolation.

(April 13, 2020)

For the Traumatized and the Departed

Dedicated to the dead and all those affected by COVID-19

The dead, all those dead have a face
A name, a history and even a legend;
They are the amiable Barber Joe
Who would cut your hair like the
Woodpecker takes on the Maple tree,
Still serving to neighborhood children
Free ice-cream on Saturday afternoons.
They are Great Samba Bosala
Or griot Mbale whose lyrical creed
And musical lore and zest gladden
Many a continent's hearts, and melancholia,
Embellishing even the Great Boredom,
Even the Great Void of being, way before
Covid ever appeared in the land.
They are Mamie Johnson, the Matriarch
Who couldn't decide between buying groceries
Or to refill her diabetic pills, torn between
Dying slowly or letting herself, in any instant,
Be ravaged by Covid's murderous, cynical fury.
They are Carmen Valle retelling the past glory
Of her ancestral Island, redeeming her people's
Mettle amid the calamities of her beloved New York.
They are Madelina, who got her first job
The day she was told of the finitude of her fate,
Her family's lightning hope of overcoming five
Hundred years on the darker side of the planet.
They are Stanley the Carpenter, affable and gentle
Always whistling as if to transcend contingence,
Lightening the load of tears and adversities.
Yes, the dead, all those dead had a face,
Their history and saga will stay ever vivid
In the museum of our passage on this Earth;
They hatched a beautiful time that was,
They have been among us, and we best celebrate
Them by making of our tears new fertilizing
Dew for the blossoming of the better part
Of us all—a new land of justice and beauty
To celebrate that which has been,
And could still be.
(May 6, 2020)

Goodbye, Aunt Lili

My aunt Marie-Ketly Robillard passed away on Sunday, May 10 (US Mothers' Day) at the age of 89, a victim of COVID-19.

My Aunt Lili, daughter of Ogoun,
Has joined the cavalcade of the departed;
Her *Ti-Bonnanj* has returned to her mythical[1]
Ginen where our ancestors retreated[2]
After valorous battles to redeem life.

My mother's longtime confidant,
Beautiful, elegant, both hopeful
In their youth wished for Haiti
A kindlier and more just future.

Ever since my embryonic conception
Aunt Lili has been a steadfast presence;
Embodiment of courage, she endured
The misery of illness while pursuing
Those delights that make life a little
Sweeter, like a song or the sun,
Perhaps a bowl of rice, *bannann peze*,[3]
A garden, a river or simply a smile.

She would want all of us to continue
The journey, steadfast, like the way
She traveled from Haiti's Kafou
To New York, Connecticut, daring
The long roads to Florida and Georgia,
Always looking forward, toward discovery
Of new horizons, new ways of reaching
Her own magnificent splendor,
Be it her grand-nephew's graduation
From storied Concord, or among companions
On the trail to life's winding slope,
Or in harmonious peace at the mountain top.

Embodiment of courage, yes, she was;
We will miss you, Aunt Lili, always.

(May 14, 2020)

Notes

1. Ti-Bonnanj (or Little good angel) is one of Haitian Vodou's two-part soul, the other part is called Gwo-Bonnanj or Big good angel.
2. Ginen is Haitian mythical original birthplace.
3. Bannann peze: fried plantain in Haitian.

From the back left: **Jill Netchinsky, Tontongi, Jonah Toussaint & my aunt Kety Robillard during a visit at her Assisting Living in Hartford**, Connecticut, in May 2019.

Fourth Period Poetics

Poems of solidarity with the suffering humanity

Where Do We Start Counting?

A poem for the black lives matter marchers. This poem is about that other pandemic of racism and dehumanization of the Other. I write it in support of the Black Lives Matter movement's fight against police brutality, structural racism, and socioeconomic disparities.

The image repels
like the spell entices
to maintain purpose.

The image repels
and impels to unveil
a new city down the valley.

The image repels
and exhorts to create
a novel covenant of the brave.

And not of appeased ardor
thrown to the zombies' pit
who can't see beyond the horizon.

It's a poem for the marchers
of all creeds, skin and colors
seeking to revive the dream.

If we must count the fallen
where do we start counting?
From Jim Crow, 1619 or 1492.[1]

Where do we start counting?
From Medgar Evers or Trayvon Martin
or the four little girls in Birmingham?

Where do we start counting?
From George Floyd, Breonna Taylor,
Ahmaud Arbery, or Fred Hampton?

It's a poem for the rainbow voices
who brave even COVID perils
to elevate the ideals of being.

"I don't preach violence, I preach equality,"
says one protester, vibrant with hope
for his country and for decency.

Also an intrepid desire to resist the bending
to the evil side of the nation's soul,
where dreams regress to nightmares.

Where do we start the tally?
From the deceits and unkept promises
or from the rebuff to widening the road?

The marchers call for the sun
to brighten landscapes untouched
neither by pain nor by the wind of history.

They want to revisit the faded memory
of Tulsa and of the "Red Summer."[2]
They want to reclaim the people's dues…

The marchers want reckoning
for misdeeds that were not named
and tales untold even in the media age.

They want answers to why humans were
made chattels in the centuries of Enlightenment?
Why statues were erected in honor of killers?

The marchers want respect and valorization
of human dignity in a kaleidoscope of freedoms.
And for injustice to no longer go unchecked.

They demand reaffirmation of what's right,
and a new narrative of justice and equality
in the everyday pursuit of one's life.

(June, 2020)

Notes

1. The dates refer to respectively the first arrival of enslaved Africans in North America in 1619 and the arrival of Columbus in the Americas in 1492.
2. "Red Summer" in reference to the many massacres of Blacks that took place from 1917 to 1923. Ibram X. Kendi, author of *Stamped From the Beginning: The Definitive History of Racist Ideas in America*, wrote that the Red Summer describes "all the blood spilled in the deadliest series of white invasions of Black neighborhoods since Reconstruction." [Source: *National Geographic*/Deneen L. Brown.

Laurels for the Dead

A Call for Peace, Dedicated to the Israeli and Palestinian Peoples

Find in your heart, my friend,
Something more soothing to say
For the advent of peace and brotherhood
Between two valiant peoples,
Unwilling relics of History,
Who have for too long suffered.

Find in your heart, my friend
The strength to deactivate your wish
For more unruly tanks to unfold
And more missiles to deploy
Along the crowded streets of Gaza
And Ramallah, en route to spreading
Internationally sanctioned terror,
Unsparing of even hospitals and patients.

Find in your heart, my friend,
The courage to undo the conquerors' work
Be it that of the Roman gladiators
Sowing dread and illusions of grandeur
Or Khalid ibn al-Walid's troops of past time
Chasing infidels and rebel tribes[1]
Find in your heart, my friend, and hear
The wake-up call from Tala Herzallah
Recounting the agony of the evacuated:
"Where are we supposed to go," she said,
"Where should I go as a civilian?
They told us to go to the South,
We went to the South,
And they bombed the South.
They told us to go to the UN schools,
And they bombed the schools.
They bombed Mosques.
The safest place in the world are hospitals
And hospitals are bombed in Gaza."[2]

Find in your heart, my friend,
The remedy to defeat pain and suffering
Deliberately induced
On other human beings,
Find the formula to keep more babies
From being cruelly machine-gunned
Under their parents' eyes, the whole world
Becoming sadistic voyeurs of mayhem.

Find in your heart, be you in Haifa
Or in Jenin, the echo of Arafat's call
To Rabin for the Peace of the Brave,
Two brother enemies turned friends
Along the river of blood and ruins;
Just like England and France
Bloody nemeses in the One Hundred Years' War[3]
Today fighting it out in soccer and rugby.

Find in your hearts, my friends,
Be you victims or aggressors
The common ground in our humanity;
Find a way to uphold while we are still alive
The torch of both immanent justice
And the transcendent affirmation of peace.
Let us find together the balance between the two.

Why would their children's bleeding
Hold less value than your children's blood
Under the same malign onslaught?
We shall all stop the cycle of defending
The means used in the name of cause or security
—O horrible means that deprave the psyche!—
Pretending to reach an uncorrupted end?
Why are festival-goers of Kibbutz Re'im forced
To pay for crimes many have probably decried?

"How to promote a non-competitive conception of
Our memory?", a writer asked himself;[4]

Couldn't one mourn the victims of the Shoah[5]
Yet still show solidarity to those of the Nakba?

Find in your hearts, my friends, the courage
To disrupt the scheduled recurrence of violence,
And uphold a fair principle of give-and-take
To live in peace what you now covet with guns;
Live our shared capacity for love, our humanity.

Oppression has its own costs, just as
Rivalry in cruelty between neighbors;
May the horrendous specter that so deeply
Invades the psyche of the peoples in pain
Find solace in the pursuit of a better way.

(Belmont, October 16, 2023)

Notes

1. "Khalid ibn al-Walid: 592–642 (Arabic: خالد بن الوليد), also known as 'The Sword of Allah', was an Arab Muslim commander [...] who

played a leading role in the Ridda wars against rebel tribes in Arabia in 632–633 and the early Muslim conquests of Sasanian Iraq in 633–634 and Byzantine Syria in 634–638. Khalid ibn al-Walid was one of the few undefeated generals in history." [Source / *Wikipedia*]

2. Laments by Tala Herzallah broadcast from Gaza by the MSNBC network (US) on October 17, 2023.

3. "Hundred Years' War, an intermittent struggle between England and France in the 14th–15th century over a series of disputes, including the question of the legitimate succession to the French crown." [Source / *Britannica*]

4. Sonia Combe, «Reconnaître les tragédies» (*Recognition tragedies*), *Le Monde Diplomatique*, October 2023.

5. *Shoah*: the Nazi holocaust of the Jews during the Second World War. *Nakba* (catastrophe): the expulsion of Palestinians from their land after the creation of the State of Israel in 1948.

How Could Your Eyes Stay Dry?

Dedicated to the Palestinian poet, activist and scholar Refaat Alareer who died on December 7, 2023, from an Israeli air strike that killed his brother, his sister and four nieces.

How could you see
so much distress and pain
the plight of the displaced
the horror on children's faces
and not be moved by the heartless
acts committed right under our gaze?

How could you see the miles
of blight, rubble, and smoke
on Gaza's desolate landscape,
the blood dried by the sun
the count of twenty thousand souls
perished in a matter of weeks
and not ask your God to say a word?

How could you see the despair,
the disparity of military might
the human beings made easy prey
by super-armed IDF lurking around
and Uncle's acquiescence and silence
and still have no tears in your eyes?[1]
How could your eyes stay dry
seeing October 7, its depravity, and all
that comes after to avenge the dead
and yet have no tears in your eyes?
How, after Abu Ghraib,[2]
could proud men be still displayed
nude on the street pavement
the world as unwilling spectator
of murderous power play in action?

How have your eyes stayed dry, tell me
what would make your humanity rise?

How could you not see empathy
as part of the liberating conscience,
part of that cry for another ethos,
that one which makes it a relief to see
the youths' refusal to inherit this war?

From the inner and far-flung cities
they refuse to take the bait for total

annihilation of the Other; they march
to the streets of Boston, Beirut,
Chicago, Rio de Janeiro, New York,
London, Amsterdam or Cairo, and cry out
for another way to uphold Right;
they call for an end to the slaughter,
they demand the initiation of mercy
in the equation for the betterment of life,
calling for ceasefire or for simple decency.

Glorious are those who refuse to be part
of this war that kills the poets, the artists,
the teachers only to be replaced by poetry,
the arts, the curiosity to go beyond,
beyond life's compressing constraints
—we shall all cry for Gaza!

(Boston, December, 2023)

Notes

1. IDF = Defense Force.
2. Abu Ghraib is a prison (and town) in Iraq that was used by US occupation forces to detain Iraqi insurgents after the US invasion of Iraq in 2003. The revelations in March 2004 of physical, sexual and psychological abuses of the detainees by US troops caused a huge and widespread scandal and international condemnation.

Columbia U Saves the Soul

Dedicated to the Columbia University students and to the students all over the US and the world who courageously stand against the politics of oppression, terrorization and annihilation of the Palestinian people pursued by the Israeli government. I have walked many times through the Columbia campus in NYC, in nocturnal, wandering promenade, with no thought of Gaza. This has forever changed.

The student bodies in encampment
are fighting for decency and elucidation
holding high the conscience of our time.

The student bodies in encampment
rebel against enmity and exclusion,
they are not about celebration of pogroms.

The student bodies in encampment
decry all anti-Jewish malevolence, the kind
of discourse of hate we saw in Charlottesville.

The student bodies in encampment demand
honesty from governments and institutions,
they demand equal rights for colonized peoples.

Instead of shallow narratives that vilify
and demonize such compassionate souls,
we shall all be proud of their intrepidity.

The student bodies in encampment
shall not be made political scapegoats
for exposing genocidal intent and act.

They are about human solidarity in motion
beauty at its peak; they represent our inner best
despite divisionary attempts to shame them.

They are about the destroyed villages, the siege,
the destruction of schools, hospitals, mosques, soup
kitchen, sudden and slow death of Gaza's children.[1]

The students are of many creeds and ethnic provenance,
a university of Muslims, Jews, Christians, Vodouists,
and Buddhists joining hands to elevate our humanity.

Repression, militarized police response, fear mongering,
efforts to harm the students' studies and future
only make the moral imperatives more urgent.

The student bodies in encampment
are about the affinities which bring us together,
human empathy in the face of horror and pain.[2]

Glory to the student bodies in encampment!
They are the hope still left in a cynical world;
they are our tomorrow, our shining light in the darkness.

(May 8th 2024)

Boston's Vigilant Watchful Eyes

In the memory of Mel King

Urban lion, eyes watchful
of our hordes' woe and pain
your 4x4 truck cruising
the Boston streets, looking
for the coalition of conscience
you called for in this dire time
I remember you, Mel.

I remember you that day, camera
in hand joining us in the Boston Common
to demand deliverance for the people
of Haiti under Tonton-Macoute reign.

I remember your joining hands
with Haitian fellows fighting
for better school in their island
for better governance of justice,
and in this land of ours all for a
better covenant under a rainbow sky;
all of us sitting around the table
in your community center, Brenda,
Daniel, Larry, Eddy, Chris, Ben, Chad
seeking your ancestral wisdom.

I remember you, Mel,
telling us that all is possible
when people's misery is the price
when human wellbeing is at stake.
Emptied of your fighting spirit
it will never be the same.

(April 2023)

Lamentations For Two Police Killings

As I was editing a poem dedicated to the killing of Sayed Faisal by Cambridge police on January 4, 2023, came the news of the deadly brutalization of Tyre Nichols on January 10. I thus combine two poems in one and dedicate it to their memory.

Part I. Sayed Faisal

Faisal was here just yesterday
a young man lost in the demons
of normality, submerged
in exhortation from all corners
to conform to one way or another.

There's demand from the Man,
and his millions of minions
then from the mental enclosure
of his far away native village
deconstructing millennia of lie-telling
mixed with western domination,
and QAnons' reinvention of facts.

Then very expectedly
come trigger-happy police,
ready-to-please strong arms
of Cantabrigian gentrification
not far from celebrated Charles River
confounding calls for intervention
with the power of life and death
while extolling the virtue of law and order.

Faisal was just yesterday
a young man with dreams
today he is a body in the mortuary;
his family, friends and hundreds of others
alarmingly outraged went to the City Hall
to ask why a life could be so cavalierly taken?

Faisal was crying for help
and was given a death sentence
expeditiously executed
like lightning in the sky
under everyone's eyes to see
regardless of pain induced
like a ritual of dehumanization
where even innocence is a commodity.

Family, friends, citizens assembled
on the people's street, our street,
demanding justice, or just human respect
along with preemptive measures
that Empire knows so well to employ
when under pressure to comply.

The protesters want to protect other lives
from trigger-happy cops hallucinating
a barbarians' invasion, terrorist threat and all,
submerged in barricading reflexes
to saving God-given neighborhoods
separating Blacks, Browns, all bodies of color
from the deserving ones, along entrenched
parameters of hate and secured paradise.

Today Faisal's family and friends
even in anguish, in the face
of such a callous deed
joined with hundreds
to call for another way,
to call for the ending
of reification of the Other
and of their use as mere pawns
in domination schemes:
We all must prevent the next killing!

Part II. Tyre Nichols

Evil has no color
it's the roots, Brother,
the machine behind the well-oiled order,
the structuration of daily routine
the brutal Black officer
as for his counterparts
of all ethnicities and creeds.

Evil has no color
it's the roots, Brother,
until Multitude says Enough!

When our tears were not yet dry
from the Cambridge killing of Faisal
came the martyrization of Tyre Nichols
and the blow to a whole community
in a vicious cycle of pain and horror.

The ordinariness of the mayhem
the casual attitude and hubris
of five police guardians
the cry of the lonely victim
for his Mama, just a few yards away
that's madness, Brother!

Memphis, Memphis, Brother,
is the house of the Master
the place where the battle
between Nature and Culture
and misconstruing reality
has taken place for all to see.

"The brutal attack on Tyre Nichols,
at the hands, the fists, the feet, the batons
of police officers"[1] beating on this man
could only revolt our conscience.

Memphis, Memphis, Brother
is not just Elvis and the blues;
it's also the demise of Martin
on a Spring day of 1968.

It's engrained conduct well programmed,
the internalization of the Code Noir[2]
it's a structural thing, Brother.

You too, my Brother

guardian of law and peace
at the forefront to suppress the human spirit
are a dupe of the imposed mirage
getting for your zeal just crumbs
to oppress and in impunity kill
your fellows of the same class or race.

Evil has no color, Brother,
it's the machinery of oppression.
May one day, O sunny and beautiful day
the collective conscience
rise up and gain the upper hand!

Notes

1. Quote from MSNBC's Ali Velshi describing the beating by the five Black police officers.
2. French for "The Black Code," a series of legal articles formulated by Jean-Baptiste Colbert in 1681 and issued by King Louis XIV in 1685 to regulate the slavery regime and the treatment of enslaved people in the colonies controlled by France.

Post-Scriptum

It was quite a spectacle to see Joe Biden, the president of the United States, condemning with such emotional outburst the killing of a Black man, Tyre Nichols, by five Memphis cops. Barack Obama showed the same verbal effusion after the killing of Trayvon Martin in 2012, going as far as saying that Trayvon could have been his son—while he didn't exert as much effort to force his Justice Department to do something about the injustice of the killing. Looking at it through a structural lens, both men sound just like mere hypocrites.

Why, despite many explosions of anger and condemnation against police killing of Black and Brown people, does it continue at such a pace? Is it, as some African-Americans, like Nikole Hannah-Jones, think, because of the direct link between the slaveholder's habit of sending posses to capture fugitive enslaved laborers and the current configuration of the police as guardians of the capitalist order?

These killings don't stay within the confines of the victims' immediate environment. They injure entire communities which bear witness. In a June 2020 statement following the murder of George Floyd, the American Medical Association (AMA) underlined the tremendous impact police violence has on the physical and mental well-being of ethnic minorities: "Police brutality in the midst of public health crises does nothing to prevent crime, it creates demoralizing conditions in an already tense period. It aggravates the psychological damage and has an obvious impact on the people around. [...] Police brutality is a stark reflection of our American heritage of racism," they said.

We must use humanist standard to measure what is acceptable in a free and democratic society governed by the rule of law and ethics. The US must find a way of making the killing of Black men and women (or any human being, for that matter) unacceptable and condemnable.

May the present poem be a gauge of my solidarity with the victims of police brutality, the suffering communities that endure it, and the struggle to end it.

Mariupol

"How do you even process those emotions?", asked
The TV anchor, moved by so much courage from
A doctor who barely escaped death when her hospital
Was blown up by an airstrike, her tone still frightened
By such incomprehensible human evil:
"A feeling of disaster," the doctor responded,
"Everything was ruined, I felt desperate,"
She said, "Everything that was dear to your life,
All your life, was ruined with this one blow…
I couldn't understand what was the fault of our patients,
The children, the doctors who were there helping…
Why was our hospital chosen to be object of the strike?"
She spoke as if she had just awakened from a nightmare
Even after one month after the lamentable event*.
The skeletal remnants of burned, solitary buildings
are haunting the endurance of our consciousness,
crying for an end to acts that cause so much suffering.
Mariupol will live to uphold all nations' right
To dream, to follow their own destinies.

The type of images the media display
From Mariupol or Bucha and from Kyiv,
Laid out in full view for us all to see
On live television or newspapers' front page,
Are overlooked when they emanate
from somewhere like Yemen or Mali or Myanmar.
We shall demand that mass killings everywhere
On our Earth be called out, exposed and reviled
In honor of human kinship and solidarity.

Tears flow from my eyes for Mariupol,
Please receive my love from Boston,
May the world come to your aid
Stay strong, O valorous Mariupol!

(April 18, 2022)

Moments in US Presidential History
(This abominable Pretender may be you)

Democracy is in harm's way, they say,
at the edge of a steep cliff
or open to possibilities that only
dreamers like MLK could marvel.[1]

Just yesterday a Trump return
was a given at RNC celebrations,[2]
today JD Vance claims the spotlight
for debasing all "childless cat ladies"
who vowed to remember come November.[3]

The two rival conventions came
and went in their grandiose ways
displaying pageantry and illusion,
the Pretender ready to take power again.

In a miracle of political dexterity
and bio-politics at its best,
the serving President, tired by Nature's
implacable process of finitude,
under unrelenting pressures
from depressed Dems seeking a way out
of the Grand Doom looming on their horizon,
finally decided to pass on to his VP the mantle.

He now made it his mission,
having swallowed his pride
to save the country from the uncertainty
of hubris and gratuitous malfeasance,
from pure animality of hate and exclusion.

The new turn has produced a new wind,
new contagious energy from a coalition
of good will converging, the ethnic
tapestry illuminating a kaleidoscope
of beauty engaged for something other than
pleonexia, facticity and the pursuit of power
for the sake of oppression and domination.[4]

In full circle surges happiness,
the Dems now exulting with new vigor
for the sudden change of fortune
and circumstance now quite joyful.

Would they blow it all up
in brotherhood bloodshed
along the line of abstraction
and egocentric madness?
Or would they seize the moment?

The Woman from Indiaribbean,
newly proclaimed holder of the lore,
told the nation why she is the chosen one;
perhaps for now the best hope for a land
so menaced by the Pretender's dangling fear,
repression — and retribution.

The Indiaribbean Woman said with a tonic
voice evoking certitude and definitude:
 "In the enduring struggle between democracy
and tyranny, I know where I stand,
and I know where the United States belongs."
Where? many downtrodden countries may ask.

Still nothing new or revelatory regarding
the on-going genocide in the Gaza Strip,
in the West Bank, in Lebanon, in Yemen;
no words on the suffering in other lands,
certainly not a sign tyranny is on the run.

Still unfazed on my part,
and asking why after a year of daily,
serial massacres and horrors
the world let this colossal mayhem
endure openly for so long;
I joined the rallies at Boston's Copley Square
crying out against such calamity brought
upon the lives of the Palestinian people.

Young and old cry out loud
in comradely eloquence "Silence is complicity!"

I envision young Haiti joining hands
of solidarity and human empathy
with Bolivar and the continental enslaved,
and even with the most Hellenic Greece,
joining in their demand to be free;
free from slave masters,
Spanish conquistadors,
and the wrath of many Empires.

Conscience and solidarity
are such boosters of hope,
and of enduring resistance,
universal concepts of redeemed value
that we shall endlessly keep
from being sullied in contempt.

Then, again this was just a dream
and my gaze now must return
to the normality of evil
and the wickedness of the process.

The abused immigrants have not missed
the direct lineage between nostalgia for power
and for a bygone mythical era,
and lynchings of centuries past,
vigilante patrols paid by the masters
to hunt the fugitive enslaved, and cops
laying low profiling all non-Whites.

Candidates to high and respected
public offices professing resentment
and contempt for others, invitation
to the madness of white supremacy.
— they never disappeared from this earth
they became more entrenched
apartheid *avant la lettre*.

"Resistance is justified,"
so goes the rally's chant
"when people are occupied."
The coalition of conscience
the whole life's mission of Jesse.[5]
It's still hard to envision
under the Great Democratic Tent
there's no place for Palestinians!
Nor for anti-hegemony thinkers.

Passing through the Harvard campus
I lament how memory can fade within
the absence and erasure of experience.
Seeing the procession of smiling
families pacing on the grass
in front of the John Harvard statue
on this first-day visit of the new students,
I can't help thinking of the profanation
of encampment protesters for Israeli divestment.
Do they know they are on holy ground?

Would the Grand Mediatic Show
be enough to dispel the threat
from the Grand Slayer of Fear
who created fear in the first place?
Arsonist turned false heroic firefighter!
Would the charm and the joy exhibited
by the newly anointed from the shadow
be enough to circumvent her complicity
in the politics of oppression in the Levant?

Fight! Fight! Fight to save democracy!
The Dems chant, rarely Fight for what is right!
Fight to see again the radiant, happy grin,
the smile of good news on the patient's face;
the chat with a neighbor under a sunny sky,
the friendly dog coming for the scraps of chicken
with great expectation and joyful patience.

Fight! Fight! Fight for what is right!
For a world where Marie LaGone can enjoy
Manuel's songs in Harvard Square while
society would afford her a nurturing space
to flourish, perhaps *regaining* her strength.

We often miss the real fight, the one
we can all win, the grand carnival of hearts,
sharing the delight of the instant.

Denuded by the Prosecutor of Amazonian
and regal allure, the Pretender was unveiled
in his true, natural, hateful state, dehumanizing
folks like his own who come to this land of refuge,
the land of thousands of sins and virtues,
the land of escape imagined by the world,
the safe harbor — the Pretender
was made the little, unimportant Napoléon
that Hugo so un-majestuously despised![6]

May the fury of the people's wrath
who, like zombies tasting salt,
have seen the road toward liberated Being
be made a conduit to a better, elevated way.[7]

If after you've seen the Pretender's rallies,
right in his element, dirt, gutter, the bait
as to who is the most hateful human being
that Mother Earth has ever produced.

Gaze of Thunder

If after the Pretender blemished the temple
of the Republic's three centennials of trials;
the great myth of the Cowboy with big heart,
Reagan calling "morning in America."

When so piously you kneel in front
of an aspirant who calls humans vermin,
glorifying his program of mass deportation,
separation of families, abandoned children
crying for their parents' return and warmth.

That person that you adore who blocks
all ways for women to take charge
of their own lives and reproductive rights,
creating unnecessary harm and suffering.

If after he claims women as prey
duly given to him by patriarchal right
you are still happy with your choice,
even after he shows his true colors?

If after the Great Debate Empire so fancies
you have seen for yourself the contrast,
you still have nostalgia for slavery time,
the time America was great, shabby and cruel?[8]

If you still promise to defend a Pretender
who would sell country, friends and family
just to satisfy his little ego and baseness.

If you would tell your own children
this person is the best of the bunch,
he who advocates for half of the country
to shame and massacre the other half,
vowing openly to wipe out all non-Whites
from this land of us all, conspiring
against humanity's safety and fate?
If you are in for all of that, perhaps
perhaps, this candidate is you.

History will certify that Black Lives Matter
was once made a cry of freedom
and for equity for all.

History will certify that the Pretender
was a real choice in a presidential contest
risking the country's destiny and image
with candidates demeaning immigrants,

the old antics of the ethnic cleansers.
This prospect is as scary as the reality
of the Pretender being the choice
of at least half of the country
— deep USA of the deep South and West
where cops and lynchers dine
inside their own bubble.

If after such a display of sympathy
for chaos and for debasement
of the whole society you would still
consent to settle on the Pretender,
welcoming him to the highest
of our institutions and aspirations,
perhaps this abominable person is you.

The Pretender and his teammate
called Haitian immigrants pet-eaters;
their peers of the past would call them
blood-sucking vampires;
even William Seabrook although[9]
a great admirer of the Vodou lore
suggested Vodouists were also cannibals.
"It's an old playbook" as VP would say,[10]
— the one inspired by US Neo-Nazis
inherited from their German brethren
who had, after all, learned it first
from their precursors the Ku Klux Klan.

May the country that comes after,
after the trials and History's wind
become the one to which we all aspire
when crossing the oceans,
along the abyssal ravines,
and climbing the steep mountains.

This is not a poem, it's a pilgrimage
along the sacred memories
from my insertion in this country.
As I mourn in this instant my departed friends
and families, they seem so meteoric,
I think of the instant that gives meaning
to the everyday formulation of life;
I think of what enlivens the psyche.

May destiny bless the United States
and Haiti too as Danticat would say.[11]

Blessed will be the people
who continue to fight
for the eclosion of new dawns
across our firmament.

At the end it wouldn't even matter
who won so coveted an election,
the whole prospect and the specter
of such a malevolent intent
hanging over humanity's head
as a Damocles sword for our time
is already here; so too is the battle
for justice and for a better world.

The people will not succumb to the abyss
of darkness for too long; faced
with depravity they refuse the binary choice,
and like birds in search of the vast unknown
they will pursue the elevation of being;
the early morning sun spreads its brilliance,
it is a beautiful day, indeed.

Notes

1. MLK: Allusion to Martin Luther King's speech at the 1963 March on Washington.
2. RNC: Republican National Convention (held in July 2024).
3. Month of the US presidential election (November, 5 2024). J.D. Vance is the Republican candidate for vice-president.
4. Pleonexia: extreme craving for greed, wealth or material possessions; avarice.
5. Allusion to Jesse Jackson, the great civil rights leader. Usual slogans and chants at anti-occupation and pro-Palestinian rallies in Boston.
6. In allusion to Victor Hugo, author of *Les Misérables,* calling Napoléon III in his collection of poems *Les Châtiments (153),* "Napoléon le petit."
7. Vodouists believe if (and when) a zombie tastes salt, he/she would regain consciousness and agency.
8. Parody of the slogan of candidate Donald Trump's movement "Make America Great Again" (MAGA).

9. William Seabrook, author of *The Magic Island,* 1929. The book is a presentation of Haitian Vodou and suggests a cannibalistic scene that was denounced as fabricated, this religion being one of the most humanist in the world.
10. VP: current Vice-President Kamala Harris. It's interesting to see how the migrants eating pets story inspired by the Neo-Nazis has quietly replaced JD Vance's anti-cat ladies story.
11. Referring to the great Haitian-American novelist Edwidge Danticat who expressed that feeling in her book Create Dangerously, The Immigrant Artist at Work (2011), when on a plane departing from Haiti.

Haiti Is Her Name

—An allegory in celebration of Haiti's independence—

She was born
against all odds
on the other side
of the long shore
amidst triangular rascality
among empires and kingdoms
the tactful puppeteers
masterfully running the game
their warships and canons
ready at their service.[1]

Her existence is a defiance
as her wounds could attest
just as her perilous mountains
reflect the mystique of her past glory.

Grand-daughter of the Mandé Charter[2]
in 13th-century Mali in agony
when human rights were first made sacred
long before the Universal Declaration
or even the Bill of Rights.
She refused the edicts of the new plantations
holding high her ancestors' quest
for justice, equality, and solidarity
the most elevated longing for freedom.

My mother compared my birthing
in a hurried taxi on a stormy night
delivered on the way to the hospital
to Haiti's accidental independence
brought about by fire, anguish, and cry
among sharks, oppressors of all kinds.
Haiti was a scandal
an ideal of being not supposed to be
something the world's masters
could neither condone nor digest.
Over two centuries in our time
she was brought to bear the rancor
of the most powerful of nations seeking
to tame her rebellious soul to keep her
from spreading beyond her frontiers and shores
her contagious freedom quest.

The world's imperials made her a pariah
to this day her children spread wide
across oceans and continents
still paying the heavy price
for her insolence and intrepidity.
She could not abide living
in chains nor taking orders
from the new Colonists and henchmen
nor reduced to the lowest state;
she couldn't endure too long
the conditioning of the mind
that would pervert the soul
to the point of folly
for only insanity and cupidity
would explain such cruelty.
She was born the rebel
that was put in quarantine,
the outcast and the trouble-maker
that disturbed the dance.
Her offspring, noble people
inspired by the spirits of their Ginen[3]
couldn't be forced to accept
this ignominious fate
even under duress and brutalization.
Alas, disunion and vile pecuniary pursuit
have overcome at times the honorable cause.
Haiti is her name
she is among the richest of nations
when evaluated for her worth
by different ontological standards
when we count the myriad of writers, poets,
storytellers, musicians, painters, sculptors,
and humanists of all stripes in her midst.
Haiti is her name
she was a miracle of existence
that only History could produce;
the French colonists' Code Noir[4]
that defined and prescribed their conduct
considered transplanted Africans
as less than a full human being
they couldn't predict the deliverance day.
Independence was not just a word
for Haiti's valorous framers
tired by years of calamity

and struggle for human dignity;
independence had a ethical dimension
attached to the infinity of possibility
humans living together in space-time
reinvented as imperative for camaraderie
in a society built on humanist foundations,
on the blossoming of a better state of being
in a beautiful world for us all to enjoy,
this is the dream that's being deferred today
—and yet still lives on.

Notes

1. Haiti gained and declared its independence on January 1st, 1804, from France following a 13-year long armed revolt launched by formerly enslaved, displaced Africans. As an advocate for enslaved people's freedom all over the world, the new country was made to become a pariah state by the powerful countries of the time (France, England, Spain, and emerging power, the United States).

2. The Mandé or Manden Charter proclaimed in 1222 in Mali is "one of the oldest constitutions in the world albeit mainly in oral form, [it] contains a preamble of seven chapters advocating social peace in diversity, the inviolability of the human being, education, the integrity of the motherland, food security, the abolition of slavery by razzia (or raid), and freedom of expression and trade." [Source UNESCO: https://ich.unesco.org/en/RL/manden-charter-proclaimed-in-kurukan-fuga-00290]

3. Ancestral, mythical homeland of the enslaved Africans and their Haitian descendants.

4. The *Code Noir* or Black Code (not to be confused with the "Black Codes" laws enacted in the US after the Civil War) was an edict proclaimed by Louis XIV in 1685 (but previously inspired by his minister Jean-Baptiste Colbert) that governed the administration of slavery in the French possessions in the Americas.

What Might Have Been

A post-election poem—

"Hey, if you can kill 20 million Native Americans, enslave 12 million Africans, and let Biden fund the slaughter of 40,000 women, children and elderly... Of course, you can install a rapist/felon/fascist as your president! In the meantime, breathe, take care of yourself, read a good book."

—*Michael Moore, film director and socio-political commentator*

It could have been
all proud daughters assembled
at the portals of Howard University
welcoming their idol in an explosion
of joy in this part of the divided nation
or simply a big show for the yearbook.

It could have been
a collective application
of Tom Paine's ideals for the USA
or a nod to Douglass and King's dreams
although Malcolm and John Brown
would have been shot out of the door
or simply a rebranding of business as usual.

It could have been
a push to encourage
community embrace
of togetherness of being,
solidarity at the level of the soul
not just the satisfaction of the gut,
or a means to enlarge the greedy elites' poll.

It could have been
a forest nourished by heaps of species
and their aspirations, their life energies
or simply a more refined gas dealer
ready to sell Alaska for a dime.

It could have been
an affirmation of respect
for the rule of law, although it's often
applied against the innocent
as many a crime bill would attest
or simply O.J. Simpson all over again.
It could have been
a statement sounding out loudly
that fascism is unacceptable

for countries supposedly civilized;
a statement proving that demeaning
other people is not a civics lesson
or simply hoping the question goes away.

It could have been
a choice for a Palestine
turned into a parking lot brought

about by expulsion or by genocide
or simply *implementing Netanyahu's*
policies and vision without his presence
—and with a friendlier smile.

It could have been
for our little girls in germination
an exemplar of equality
their value being accepted
as universal in our Multiverse
or a paradise of liberated women
as dreaded by the US Supreme Court.

It could have been
also most certainly
adoption of Ivy-League concepts
as planetary ethos and edicts
though humans are more complex
ven the most moronic among us
or simply redoubled State control
camouflaged as need for security
and of peace of mind undisturbed.
It could have been
an opportunity to honor and welcome
a woman at the helm of public affairs
just like it's been for millennia
in other parts of our world
or establishing along the Potomac
an imperial Wonder Woman presidency.

It could have been
a statement of rejection
of the billionaires' vision
of a pre-civil rights USA
when patriarchy ran amok
and whiteness was the paradigm,
the elemental essence of being
—or believing change is already here.

It could have been
the reign of a Black Hilary Clinton
instead of that of an unhinged fascist,
the wink to the colors' ghettos
with a semblance of Christian love,
the reversal of the urge to isolate
and exclude instead of the process
to non-being until the next revolt
or simply screaming USA! USA! USA!
It could have been
the beginning of a new road
instead of a dead-end of hatred
or a fake terrestrial redemption
under CNN's spotlight of heroes.

However dark our realities
and blurry our paths might be
we must always create
even in adversity and desolation
spaces for the hatching
of multiple ways of being
spaces for displaying
our multiple splendors.

(Boston, December 2024)

Moments in Neo-Nero's Return

(Dedicated to Michèle Voltaire Marcelin)

"This is Not Normal," said Congresswoman Melanie Stansbury's protest sign during Donald Trump's first joint session of Congress address on March 4, 2025. Indeed, we're living at a different level of consciousness, in a dual reality that, sometimes, only poetry can capture.

Amidst the unveiled darkness
unfolding over the land
fear ridden in color of anxiety
and the buffoons running the show
I can still find beauty in the day.

As I departed this morning
for a long day at the office
hugging goodbye to Jill
sensing the gusty chill outside,
her smile radiating in the room,
I said, relaying Jesse's mantra:
"Let's keep hope alive!"[1]

The Vandals' tentacles have reached
across oceans and continents,
damning every evidence of horror
blaming Ukraine for her own agony,
in Russia's war of conquest
sacrificing her cause
for the sake of vanity
and imperial voracity
sane-washing Putin,
infantilizing his missiles
while making Haiti,
unsung mother of South America,
the specter of the inconceivable.
Hell is now englobing
both our Haiti and our USA.

In a daily dosage of hate,
dehumanization of others and self,
Dr. Phil in tow, microphone
in hand, CNN and Fox News exuberant
while pain becomes spectacle
for a country quasi zombified,
dismembered at the altar of egomania,
avarice elevated as State religion
while the bastards toast to our anguish.

In any other country or time
this fruit would have been ripe
for an uprising or a huge proclamation
for the redemption of our humanity.

Where was your ancestry when
Christopher Columbus invaded this land?
Why have the refugees of yesteryear
braving ravaging seas and mountains of perils
in time changed to New Age Goebbels
turning propaganda advisor
for the project of Mass Deportation
of all deemed Black or Brown
in this United States of Amerikkka?

This horrible thing
in your daily watch
is no illusion, brother,
it's the real thing,
the old time, millenary plan
for debasement of Being
which only the multitude
and those left in the arid desert
can defeat and surpass while
planting flowers along the river's path.

Real lives of everyday people
living under fear and chagrin,
lives of social security recipients
of the homeless on the street corner
of the civil servants humiliated,
impoverished for the sake of billionaires'
tax cuts, and immigrants suffering in silence
while the arrogant rich are calling the shots,
aligning with Southern White Supremacists
from whom the Nazis learned their trade.

It's nothing new, my friends,
under this sun that rarely faded;
it's the lesson learned by our ancestors
on the plantations, and yet one day
the enslaved Haitians showed
that hope can emerge from the ashes.

It's the lesson sweatshop workers
and indigents of all kinds had long learned,
although not too often practiced;

it's the lesson of the Bastille masses
taking destiny into their own hands;
it's the storming of the Winter Palace
brave spirits calling for a new dawn.

Let's call the cat a cat
which name he proudly claims;
let's name the nature of the beast
the only condition to tame its fury.[2]

In the meantime the migrants,
useful and apropos scapegoats
are left in their miseries,
some living the odyssey
as tracked animals in the urban jungle
or deported to their fate
in the wilderness of oblivion
exposing Western civilization's
hypocrisy and moral neglect.

Yes, the struggle continues
to each generation its own challenges;
nothing is given for keeps;
our aim is the elevation of Being,
human dignity reaching its highest point;
just as our hearts' paths,
opening new roads.
It's Revolution, my friends, both
a challenge and a dream.

These are onerous times
for awakened consciences to absorb
the resurgence of tyrannical instinct
in your face and on such a grand scale
reminiscent of when the crematorium
directors and enslaved's masters of all kinds
held power over our destinies.

It's even more regrettable
that so many of our great poets
and moral voices for our time
have lately departed our landscape, while
the scoundrels seize the upper hand.[3]

As I marveled at the geometrical design
of the snow's magical spread
along normally ordinary streets

transformed into eerie new space,
I wondered if there's anything, advice
or lesson, the Gazaans could learn
from this land's first inhabitants
as their own is being offered to neocolonists
as a stolen Riviera of the Middle East.

"This show is tragically clownish,"[4]
said the media observer, seeing the sole
billionaire's gig like an extraterrestrial
directing State affairs like his little playthings.

In the fury to apply their Project[5]
the Vandals have violated even
the ethics of the First Amendment
trampling long honored conventions
laws and treaties that protected human rights
crushing the simple decency of respect.[6]

The assaults against fairness
at the expense of decency
are unbearable for creators of meaning
those who pursue the highest attainment
of human integrity, as for any human being.

It is incumbent upon all of us,
witnesses of abomination,
to join in the great struggle
to reanimate the lifeless cadaver
mindful as History has shown
it can reappear transformed
in the jubilation of a renewed humanity.

As I walk along the road
paved with the second layer
of white, fluffy snow
the hibernated branches
of the trimmed maple tree
fighting carelessly the elements,
I'm reminded we're in the heart
of an ethical meltdown,
the reins of State captured
by the most malicious hands
of self-interested Vandals
of twenty-first century vintage;
only a huge upheaval of defiance
could vanquish such calamity.

Overtaken by deep thoughts
on the snow's redeeming qualities,
its beauty relativizing New England's
schizophrenic winter chill,
once again I found attraction
in the abstraction of evil,
fighting it became a fate I cannot avoid,
in that moment, even the cold, freezing air
now, suddenly, is lived with delight.

(March 2025)

Notes

1. In reference to civil rights leader Jesse Jackson who likes to proffer this slogan in rallies for human rights.
2. In allusion to French philosopher Jean-Sartre's famous postulate that "Naming is changing" (in the sense that naming the thing for what it is unveils it to critical apprehension, therefore making it possible to change it—and not be fooled by it).
3. In reference to fallen cultural giants Nikki Giovani (December 9, 2024), Max Manigat (December 23, 2024), Jimmy Carter (December 29, 2024), Danielle Legros Georges (February 11, 2025), Franketienne (February 20, 2025), and Anthony Phelps (March 11, 2025), who passed away in the period of four months since Trump's November 5 election.
4. This quotation is from MSNBC's broadcaster Chris Hayes on his show "All In" aired February 27, 2025.
5. In reference to "Project 2025," the neo-fascistic project, with totalitarian overtones and manipulated religious fervor, that seeks to "deconstruct" the apparatus of the administrative state, pressing for a complete right-wing overhaul of the US sociopolitical system. For reference, check the Heritage Society's text, *Project 2025: Building for conservative victory through policy, personnel and training*.
6. This stanza was inspired by Mahmoud Khalil arrestation, the pro-Palestinian civil rights activist, Columbia University graduate student and green card holder that the State Department is trying to deport because of his protests against the Gaza genocide. It also encompasses the extra-judicial arrest or kidnapping of Tufts doctoral student, Fulbright scholar , and student visa holder Rumeysa Ozturk, presumably for adding her name to an anti-Israel editorial in a student newspaper—and, of course, the US' recent withdrawal from international treaties and conventions such as the Paris Climate Accord and the World Health Organization.

Epilogue in Three Parts

Fascism's Specter, Alienation and Self-Mutilation

I. The Bull and the Red Cape

In a fairer system of government, the $1 million-a-day voter sweepstakes that Elon Musk's political action committee organized and offered to poor voters in the swing states, should have constituted a violation of electoral law. Given the crucial role of Pennsylvania and the swing states in the electoral, mathematical contest of 2024 (regardless of other voter-suppression shenanigans that occurred in the red or Republican-controlled states particularly in communities of color and lower income voters), it's clear that this act successfully impacted the election in favor of Trump.

The reality is that the deadly mixture of racism, misogyny, xenophobia, greed, and alienation has carried the day in the United States presidential election of 2024. If I were organizing a presidential contest of candidates who don't want to be president, there wouldn't be a better candidate than Donald Trump. He had done everything necessary to disqualify him or to make him unattractive to voters. The *Vanity Fair* magazine cover of November 6, 2024 says it all: "34 Felony Counts, One Conviction, 2 Cases Pending, 2 Impeachments, 6 Bankruptcies, 4 More Years, The 47th American President." Without mentioning the litany of insults and vulgarities Trump spread around against his opponents up to the last hours of the campaign.

Evidently, people's emotions and desire for change (or even entertainment) were manipulated with great success by the Trumpian propaganda machine, aided by the oligarch billionaire Elon Musk and his two billion subscribers on X (the Musk-purchased social media platform formerly known as Twitter). Voters were fed a copious menu of conspiracy theories and outright lies—not to mention foreign services using manipulative techniques to instill fear and mutual hatred among the US populations.

Cases in point were the fabricated stories about Haitians eating dogs and cats, Venezuelans' so-called powerful gangs sowing terror in US-American cities and villages, invasions by hordes of menacing immigrants, etc., all to foster an environment of fear of the Other that serves well the disseminators of the falsehoods.

Although the choice of Donald Trump, a candidate who advocates an open preference for hateful methods and ideology, says as much about the country and its voters, on another level I understand how people from the working and downtrodden classes may have voted for Trump as a rejection of a sociopolitical system that has let them down, creating illusory value systems that devalue both their productive and existential worth. For these voters, Trump is a vehicle, a useful instrument to get back at a system that excludes and exploits them. The lyrical expressions and exhortations to "save democracy" the Democrats lavished on the electorate didn't mean anything to them; they would vote for the Devil himself if it gave them leverage to stick it to what they perceive as the "elites", the urban and suburban educated and techno-financial classes that control the economy and large sectors of the mass media. In the past, many of those working-class electors might have voted Communist.

There are also, of course, influential voters and donors of the wealthy, billionaire class, motivated exclusively by greed and the imperative of control and power; for them, ethics, the suffering of Others, the graciousness of civic duties, generosity toward another human being, have no value at all. The fight for change must be directed toward those. For the others, political education and a praxis of what I would call *humanist engagement*—advocacy for a better world, for better schools, better medical coverage, care for the environment, comradery with neighbors, and so forth—would be a good approach.

The discourse of multiethnicity, cultural pluralism, and of inclusion espoused by Vice President-turned Democratic presidential candidate Kamala Harris and her campaign rang hollow when they refused to let Palestinian-American representatives address the Democratic National Convention in August 2024, while allowing Israeli representatives to do so. This throwing cold water on the "joyful" ambiance by the campaign may have been one of the consequential "missed opportunities" that the Democrats failed to recognize. Showing respect and some measure of solidarity toward a people facing ongoing genocide by a powerful army—while respecting US obligations to its alliance with Israel—would have been the right thing to do.[1]

No, it's not economic anxiety alone that explains the embrace by the electorate of Trump's imbecilic non-program that relied on fear, exploitation of people's hardships, hatred of "different" human beings, male dominance, patriarchal prerogatives, and the super-rich minority's immorality and greed.

There are certainly other factors that led people to choose, faced with a binary choice between a highly qualified woman—Hillary Clinton in 2016, Kamala Harris in 2024—and "the most unqualified man"—Donald Trump in 2016 and 2024—voting for the latter,[2] ignoring all factors of disqualification, including vulgarities, fraud, the demeaning of others, sowing race hatred, causing physical and emotional harm to vulnerable people, etc. These are all traits a healthy citizenry wouldn't normally want in its president

To the Trump voters, I would say: Perhaps you should reconsider how you accomplish your civic duty of voting, how it should relate to the plight of your community, to its longing for better conditions of living for all, toward its *complétude*, its completeness of being. Alienation is not a form of virtue. To use a metaphor of the great Haitian poet and storyteller Jean-Claude Martineau, let's all root for the bull to eventually recognize there's someone behind the toreador's red cape, and that it: *Was in the end only an instrument / In a last effort of its eyes / Veiled in dust and blood / The bull discovers the toreador.*[3]

Indeed, behind the red cape there are the architects of Project 2025, who want to overhaul the entire US federal system to benefit a retrograde political ideology. In this respect, the reelection of Donald Trump may mark a departure from a democratic capitalism with the presumption of civic good to that of an instinctual, Nazi-friendly capitalism, society's being subjected to the whims of billionaires and their minions of the political, white-supremacist class.

Before the election, I was of the belief that the United States had attained such a high stage of political development and moral maturity that it would, ultimately, *not* re-elect a person like Donald Trump. Obviously, I was wrong.

After the election, knowing the rhetoric and policy proposals the Trump campaign advocated, I returned once more to Daniel J. Goldhagen's book *Hitler's Willing Executioners—Ordinary Germans and the Holocaust* (1996), to comprehend the United States of 2024: How ordinary people, accustomed to democratic rule and principles, could choose fascism by means of free choice and agency. This irony is evident in Donald Trump's reelection. It also shows the actualization of the excellence of manipulative techniques in real time. It shows how a mediocre TV character, hyped up by the media, and expertly packaged as an agent of change, can create illusory inferences that impose upon reality to the point of electing him president of the United States!

We may feel that we are far from the European pogroms of 1930s–1940s, but it is wise to remember that ordinary people can contribute to the ordinary process of evil: "[T]hey could slaughter whole populations—especially populations that are by any objective evaluation not threatening—out of conviction," as Goldhagen observes in *Hitler's Willing Executioners,* lamenting that "the historical record, from ancient times to the present, amply testifies to the ease with which people can extinguish the lives of others, and take joy in their deaths."[4] Mass deportation, mass induction of pain or mass dehumanization, is not that far from mass extermination, after all: it sometimes starts with the first (one of President-elect Trump's campaign promises).

It's not only recent immigrants who feel the trepidation of this election. Gays, trans people, women, and the majority of people of color are affected, as well. Women of all races in this country see, in the incoming administration, the assault against their reproductive rights, the patriarchal machismo and misogyny in action. Black women, who saw Harris's candidacy as a conduit to breaking the glass ceilings of both race and gender, feel devastated by the idea of a Trump administration. Waikinya Clanton, founder of the organization Black Women for Kamala said to a *New York Times* reporter: "This isn't a loss for Black women, it's a loss for the country. America has revealed to us her true self, and we have to decide what we do with her from here."[5]

What to do with this country is to engage in civic questioning, willing to tell truth to power, participating in the collective discourse, in the pursuit of humanist finality. Many may feel the election as the end of a road. Even in the worst-case scenario where Trump would institute a dictatorship, I would remind people that there is always life during and after a dictatorship, or any authoritarian regime for that matter—see what has happened just this week in Syria.[6]

History—as the varied history of the United States itself attests—is cyclical, with good and bad times, but the sun always returns to the horizon, always open to new possibilities, new ways to realize the future while enjoying the present, with all its contingencies and spaces for grace.

—Tontongi (This text is extracted from a longer text published in the magazine *Tanbou* in November 2024.)

Notes

1. On the question of genocide, see Amnesty International report: "Amnesty International investigation concludes Israel is committing genocide against Palestinians in Gaza": https://www.amnesty.org/en/latest/news/2024/12/amnesty-international-concludes-israel-is-committing-genocide-against-palestinians-in-gaza/.
2. MSNBC news anchor Joy Reid made this point on November 6, 2024, the day after the election.
3. Jean-Claude Martineau, a.k.a. Koralen, *Flè Dizè*, (Boston 1978). English translation by us.
4. Daniel Jonah Goldhagen, *Hitler's Willing Executioners—Ordinary Germans and the Holocaust*, (Alfred A. Knopf, 1996).
5. Erica Green and Maya King, "For Black Women, 'America Has Revealed to Us Her True Self'", (*New York Times*, November 7, 2024).
6. Allusion to the early December, 2024, political convulsion in Syria, when the Syrian rebel group Hayat Tahrir al-Sham (HTS), led by AÅbu Mohammad al-Jolani, seized the capital Damascus and overthrew the longtime dictatorship of Bashar al-Assad who fled to Russia.

From the left: **Denizé Lauture, Tontongi & Max Manigat in Cambridge, Massachusetts, for a reading in Homage to Paul Laraque** (Boston, MA) in 2002.

II. On Anticipatory Obedience

In the weeks leading up to the US presidential election of November 5, 2024, many critics used historian Timothy D. Snyder's terms "anticipatory obedience" to refer to the tendency of some personalities in the political class, in the media and the public at large to withdraw criticisms or comments that they deem displeasing to Trump and his MAGA movement—obviously not to anger a candidate who promises "revenge" and "retribution" to anyone he considers a potential enemy.

The self-preservation reflex not to upset Trump's thin skin susceptibility and his myriad gun-toting supporters got real and became more pervasive as the country approached the final days of the election. Instances of the anticipatory obedience reflexes were evident, for example, in the decision by the anchors of the usually Democrat-leaning MSNBC cable news show Morning Joe—Joe Scarborough and Mika Brzezinski—to visit Trump at his Florida country-club domicile Mar-a-Lago in the wake of the election. Critics of Trump, they hardly hid the fact they were motivated by anticipation of Trump's retaliation toward them.

Another example of *anticipatory obedience* is the planned separation of MSNBC and CNBC from NBC (part of the "reorganization" of parent corporation Comcast). Lee Petro, a Washington DC lawyer following the trend, says that any application review by the upcoming Trump administration might "cause pain" to NBC. The rationale: MSNBC being an antenna of anti-Trump opposition, distancing oneself from it seems like a healthy policy. "It's hard not to look at the spinoff of CNBC and MSNBC as potentially a response to the new administration," concluded Petro.[1]

The *anticipatory obedience* to authoritarianism can also be observed in the public at large, in the mundanity of every day's people in action. I observed it on my social media where very few of my "friends" "liked" posts or reports where I showed support for Palestinian rights or when I criticized Trump. People's first reflex is for self-preservation.

Ian and Maximilian Potter, who examined Trump's public statements and actions by the US government and the media, say in the *Columbia Journalism Review*: "We fear that, despite the conventional wisdom that American media independence survived the tests of Trump's first term unscathed, developments in the years since he left office tell a different story. That story is that, like Orbán's, Trump's campaign against the media has taken time to have its intended effect, but have an effect it has, and the trajectory discernible now, in hindsight, doesn't bode well for the media."

They cite Prof. Timothy Snyder's book, *On Tyranny,* in which he coined the concept "anticipatory obedience" to define such behavior from people living under dictatorship: "Most of the power of authoritarianism is freely given. In times like these, individuals think ahead about what a more repressive government will want, and then offer themselves without being asked. A citizen who adapts in this way is teaching power what it can do."

To understand billionaire entrepreneur Jeff Bezos's decision not to let the *Washington Post* endorse any presidential candidates this year, although they have done so for many decades, one need only view it in the context of 2016, eight years earlier. Here's what Ian and Maximillian Potter write regarding that moment: "As CNN and the Post continued to report on Trump in ways he did not like, he openly threatened that, if elected, he would seek revenge against them. At a rally in early 2016, he called out Amazon and its founder, Jeff Bezos, owner of the Post, and said: "If I become president, oh do they have problems. They're going to have such problems.""[2]

It's in the same vein, seen in the context of past dealings with Donald Trump (having experienced his willingness to use Federal government power for personal use and to exact revenge), that one should understand the media's accommodation for him and his normalization—or what 's lately being called "sane-washing"—as an acceptable political figure. One clear example was CNN's town hall-style interview featuring anchor Kaitlan Collins and Donald Trump on May 11, 2023, giving him a huge propaganda platform to disseminate his lies and venomous rhetoric.

Other examples of covertly expressed complicity in the normalization of Trump or non-problematization of Trump's public statements include the *New York Times*' and *Washington Post*'s treatment of General John Kelly's report of Trump's praise for Adolf Hitler, his suggestion that Hitler too "did some good things." These "newspapers of record" could have treated it as a more urgent and compelling story.

Besides anti-Trump parlance, another topic where anticipatory obedience reflexes are at play is the Palestinian question. Given the enormous power of the Israeli government lobby in the United States, those who don't let themselves be intimidated by its power to censure or self-censure, usually end up with multiple problems on their hands. One remembers the examples of *Claudine Gay, Liz Magill* and *Sally Kornbluth*, respectively presidents of Harvard University, University of Pennsylvania and MIT, who did not give the answer wanted by the conservative NY Congresswoman Elise Stefanik during a Congressional hearing regarding antisemitism on US campuses.

The latest example, at the time of writing, is the banning of MIT's linguistics professor Michel DeGraff from teaching in his own department where he's worked for 28 years. In a petition released by MIT students to support DeGraff, who is of Haitian descent, they wrote: "We scholars, journalists, and people of conscience stand in full solidarity with *Written Revolution* chief editor Prahlad Iyengar and Linguistics Professor Michel DeGraff as they face targeted attacks, bans, and unjust punitive action from MIT."

Prof. DeGraff's supporters denounced the "institutional violence" to which MIT has resorted to punish the activists: "In both Prahlad Iyengar's and Professor Michel DeGraff's cases, MIT has enacted serious and long-lasting punitive measures without due process, a continuation of a larger trend of rushing to penalize those speaking, writing, and acting in solidarity with Palestine without evidence of clear policy violations, " they deplored.

The tragedy of the horrific Israeli violence that fell (and continues to fall today, over a year later) upon the Palestinian people since the Hamas massacres of Israelis on October 7, 2023, is an occurrence of gigantic proportions for humanity's conscience. Many a time have I lamented the quasi-absence of US poets, as a collective voice, in the fight against the decades-long Israeli occupation of Palestinian territories. Unlike the Palestinian poets who, as members of civil society, as engaged citizens and everyday companions in life's pursuit, have always used poetry—with its inherent nature of transcendence and alterity of seeing, feeling and being—as an important protagonist in the Palestinian resistance. Since the 1980s until his death in 2008, the great Palestinian poet Mahmoud Darwish affirmed Palestinian existence with cry and alarm, appealing equally to the common sense of humanity, the common rejection of the application of crude fascism, crude force, crude genocidal sadism.

In a recent post on *my social media* I lamented that I "*missed the time when poetry had a consciousness.*" It was a comment regarding a group photo from a poetry reading some ten years ago that displayed, among others, the great liberation poets Askia Touré, Brenda Walcott, Aldo Tambellini, Everett Hoagland, Jill Netchinsky, Ashley Rose Salomon, Neil Callender, and this author. I intended the comment to be provocative and controversial. Naturally, poetry—being an elemental and fundamental expression of human existence and affect—has certainly never ceased to have a "consciousness". My point was to outline clearly my dissatisfaction with non-Palestinian poets (or non-Ukrainian poets for that matter) who don't express outrage at horrors committed on their watch, if not in their names.

Should poetry be political? It cannot afford not to be. Should poetry be a pawn in the service of a political party or ideology? The answer to that is definitely no. Should poetry be politically engaged on the side of the oppressed? Absolutely yes! That's exactly when its natural, transcendental essence comes into play.

Notes

1. See Matt Egan, "The fate of MSNBC could be in Trump's hands", CNN November 21, 2024: https://www.cnn.com/2024/11/21/business/msnbc-trump-comcast-cnbc/index.html
also see https://finance.yahoo.com/news/happen-cnbc-msnbc-no-longer-050902674.html
2. Ian and Maximillian Potter "On anticipatory obedience and the media", Columbia Journalism Review, October 2024: https://www.cjr.org/analysis/anticipatory-obedience-bassin-potter-scheppele-orban-trump-hungary-media-punish.php

III. Poetry as Resistance

It is almost an oxymoron to say "political poet" as we generally say of so-called poètes engagés or politically committed poets, to the extent that Poetry (with a capital P) permeates and is permeated by the entire ambient social and political order. As an expression of the depth of human affect and sensitivity, in relation to what it perceives as fallen within categories of beauty and ugliness, and in relation to environmental phenomena, Poetry gives to itself the mission to reveal Reality. It says the unsaid and the unsayable, because it knows, like Jean-Paul Sartre, that "to name is to change".

Poetry says the *unsayable* hidden behind societal rituals and, since at least the advent of Surrealism, seeks to reinvent the order of classical, ancestral epistemologies, get rid of language's applied functionality, reveal the hidden riches of the intellect. Because of all this, Poetry participates in the political sphere which, through all civilizations created by the various human tribes, governs daily life, at times giving it meaning and direction.

Those who think poetry is innocent should ask the tyrants why they take it so seriously. Ask the early 20th century Haitian dictator, Nord Alexis, why he ordered the execution of Massignon Coicou, the great Haitian poet, actor and playwright. To establish both the fearsome and mystical aspects of the execution, the government of Alexis ordered a semi-religious horseback procession of the execution team, in the middle of the night. The procession, all in silence, headed to the cemetery of Port-au-Prince, where Coicou and two of his brothers, Horace and Pierre-Louis, plus twenty other anti-Alexis insurgents, were summarily executed on the night of March 14 to 15, 1908 in front of the exterior walls of the Port-au-Prince cemetery.[1]

François Duvalier (Papa Doc) would do the same thing, more than half a century later, in the execution of Louis Drouin and Marcel Numa on November 12, 1964, this time in broad daylight, in front of the west side of the cemetery of Port-au-Prince. They were the last survivors of the thirteen members of the anti-Duvalierist group Jeune Haiti or Young Haiti who landed in Dame-Marie, Haiti, in August 1964, to launch guerrilla warfare against Duvalier's bloodthirsty dictatorial regime.

***

If you asked the greatest of our international poets— those especially called political poets, such as Vladimir Mayakovsky, Paul Éluard, Louis Aragon, Pablo Neruda, Jacques Roumain, Emma Lazarus, Langston Hughes, Amiri Baraka, Paul Laraque, Marielle Franco or Benjamin Zephaniah—if you asked them why they were so concerned about Politics (with a capital P), they would probably have laughed in your face. More seriously, they would have also told you that they felt they had no choice.

The poets of Gaza today, for example, have no choice either, as they find themselves targets of Israeli genocidal aggression. Alongside their families under attack, Palestinian poets express the depth of their souls; they, together with the journalists, the doctors, the teachers, and the rest of the civilians, are paying the ultimate price for their resistance.

Israel's war against Hamas in the Gaza Strip (over more than a year-long today as I am writing) has reaffirmed the intrinsic link between Poetry and Resistance, if only by the sheer numbers of Palestinian journalists and poets killed there by the bombardments of the Israeli invading forces. Among the casualties are Omar Abu Shaweesh, poet, novelist, and community activist, who was killed at his home in Nuseirat camp on October 7, 2023 by an Israeli airstrike; Heba Abu Nada, poet, novelist and educator, killed at her home in Gaza on October 20, 2023, by an Israeli airstrike, and many, many others. Among them the renowned poet, novelist, and educator Refaat Alareer: he was killed in Gaza, also by an Israeli bombardment, along with his brother, his sister and his four nieces on December 7, 2023. A few days before his death, he wrote in a premonitory poem entitled "If I must die," the following salient lines:

If I must die,
you must live
to tell my story
to sell my things
....
so that a child, somewhere in Gaza
while looking heaven in the eye
awaiting his dad who left in a blaze—
and bid no one farewell
....
If I must die
let it bring hope
let it be a tale.[2]

Naturally, Alareer was in no way supposed to die, except for the fact that the Israeli retaliation to avenge the deadly Hamas attack of October 7, 2023 went beyond the scope of mere "retaliation" to become downright genocidal. The annihilation of a people, right under the glare of the whole world to see. The great Jewish-Israeli poet and professor of Hebrew, Natan Zack, who died in 2020 at the age of 89, demonstrated that poetry can transcend national boundaries and ideologies. He strongly supported Palestinian liberation, going so far as voicing support for the group of activists who, in May 2010, used a flotilla of six vessels to penetrate the Israeli blockade of the Hamas-controlled Gaza Strip. Had he been still alive, he probably would have condemned both the horrendous Hamas attack of October 7 and the genocidal Israeli response.

Examples of poetry as resistance against oppression abound across the globe and across time

A poet is like a bird that defies the impositions of gravity; he or she transcends the confining societal norms, questioning intent and behaviors. Poets know the trap of censorship, especially self-censorship, which is another way of doing the oppressors' work, without showing their hands. Many poets end up being killed, imprisoned or made social pariahs.

In November 2003, The British-Jamaican poet Benjamin Zephaniah angrily rejected an invitation from the Queen of England to Buckingham Palace to accept a coveted OBE award in the name of the Order of the British Empire. In explaining his rejection of the award, Zephaniah denounced Britain's participation in the war against Iraq and British colonialism in general. He said that the Order reminded him of "thousands of years of brutality—[and] how my foremothers were raped and my forefathers brutalized.[3]" It is clear that those at the helm of governments or societal organization of life clearly understand the political significance of Poetry. When Señora Rosales asked Ruiz Alonso, the head of the fascist Falangist squad that came to arrest the Spanish poet Federico García Lorca on the fateful afternoon of August 16, 1936, what Lorca had done to deserve such a fate, Alonso responded: "He's done more damage with a pen than others have with a pistol."[4] Beside Lorca's anti-fascist writings, the Falangists couldn't stomach Lorca's gay lifestyle, nor his portrayal of the Romani people as equal if not superior. To show gratitude for the Black vote that helped him win the White House, President-elect Bill Clinton invited poet and author Maya Angelou to read at his 1993 inauguration, giving her a huge exposure and himself an important symbolic representation, especially useful after Clinton's slighting of African-American pop-rap singer Sister Souljah during the 1992 presidential campaign. Before Clinton, John F. Kennedy convinced Robert Frost to read at his 1961 inaugural. Both Kennedy and Clinton were Democratic party candidates whose elections followed long reigns of Republican administrations; hence the insurgent character of their inaugurals. Both cases, however, also represent the prostitution of poetry by a powerful government institution.

Unlike Frost and Angelou, Robert Lowell didn't see the need to flatter or let himself be flattered by the powers that be. Many of Lowell's poems are testimonials to his life as a citizen-artist whose political activism is an important part of his being. Disturbed by the Allied bombing of civilians in Dresden and other German cities during the Second World War, he became a conscientious objector, which landed him in jail for several months.

In 1965, Lowell indignantly rejected an invitation from Kennedy's successor Lyndon Johnson to a White House Arts Festival, denouncing the United States' escalation of the war in Vietnam. He was among the thousands who joined the anti-war March on the Pentagon in October,

1967. In fact, while most of Lowell's poetry is not overtly political, his life is a celebration of freedom and dissent, in the tradition of Charles Baudelaire in France or Massillon Coicou in Haiti.

Lowell's rejection of royal flattery is echoed by many other poets of great influence who have rejected awards on grounds of principle. In 1994 the Russian poet Yevgeny Yevtushenko refused an award given to him by then president Boris Yeltsin, in protest of the Chechnya war; Yevtushenko criticized the war in Iraq as well.

Poets Against the Second Iraq War

Faced with the growing militarization of everyday life under the administration of George W. Bush, which became more and more belligerent following the terrorist attacks of September 11, 2001, some of us in Cambridge and Boston founded a group of poets that we coined Liberation Poetry Collective. In our Mission Statement, we declared:

"We are a group of writers and educators from diverse ethnic, socio-economic and cultural provenances who joined hands on January 1st, 2001, to propagate the ideals we attach to poetry: that it can be a potent agent for change while enlightening and entertaining the soul. For us, poetry and the liberation from exploitation and oppression are not two parallel entities, but rather an organic whole, one tightly woven endeavor. Given that even poetry cannot live completely outside the materiality of human experience, we believe that solidarity with and among peoples is at the core of the praxis of being. Our completeness depends upon our continual search not only for beauty and elation, but also for justice, for respect of the integrity of the Other, for equality of all human beings."

We continued, feeling the need to be exact:

"Liberation poetry is liberation of the soul, the rejection of one-dimensional, disfiguring post-modernist fads. We will tell the children the truth, as Bob Marley intoned, but we also open ourselves to learn from them. If our objective is to bring poetry to the streets, as Brenda Walcott suggests, then our poets will work with all peoples, embracing the rejected and the disenfranchised, learning to expose and to resist the mechanisms of political oppression and cultural mystification."

Now, satisfied by the liberation insight of our position, we concluded, unflinching:

"We are the new visionary warriors, the new maroons, and our creed is one of human affirmation. We aim to launch a cultural insurrection that brandishes and celebrates poetry as a powerful weapon for resistance against degradation, in the pursuit of human freedom and justice. "

That statement, dated January 2002, was signed by Tontongi, Jill Netchinsky, Brenda Walcott, Aldo Tambellini, Askia Touré, Anna Wexler, and Gary Hicks. It is published in the anthology *Poets Against the Killing Fields* (Boston: Trilingual Press, 2003).

In the Introduction to that anthology, I mentioned some of the poets who, historically, took issue against oppression or what they perceived as societal wrongdoings:

"Indeed, before and after the second Iraq war was launched, many poets registered their dissent in writing or marching. In February 2003 Laura Bush, the wife of the president, canceled a poetry symposium that was to take place at the White House, out of concern that the gathering would be used by the poets to promote antiwar feelings. If anything, the panicked cancellation of the poetry symposium by the White House demonstrates a deeply seated fear of poetry as dissent, capable of inflicting tremendous practical damage. In response to the White House's cancellation, hundreds of poets joined together in Manchester, Vermont, in a sort of counter symposium titled "A Poetry Reading to Honor the Right of Protest as a Patriotic and Historical American Tradition." The poets denounced the White House's cowardice, and called for the prevention of the war against Iraq. They eventually published an anthology, *Cry Out: Poets Protest the War, the written product of the Manchester gathering*."[5]

"When our public reading group, The Liberation Poetry Collective, organized a 'Cabaret for Peace' in Cambridge, Massachusetts, in December 2002, to counteract Georges W. Bush's preparation for war against Iraq, it was with the conviction that this war plan was an imperialist and wrongful enterprise, and that poetry is a legitimate instrument for dissent against war. Again in May, 2003, two months after the launching of the war, we organized a forum on 'Poetry for Resistance and Liberation,' and later, a series of readings under the theme 'Poets against the Killing Fields'—in response to the atrocities in Fallujah and Najaf, and the continued killings of Palestinians by Israeli occupation forces, and that of Israeli civilians by the Palestinian resistance—it was at once a manifestation of dissent against the US warmongers, an expression of solidarity with an oppressed people, and a cry for liberation of the human spirit."[6]

Failing, however, despite the many antiwar demonstrations, to keep the war from getting started, we joined with the efforts of many in the US and abroad who wanted it to stop, stop its spread, stop its atrocities and its plethora of crimes against humanity. In a June 25, 2004, in a statement inviting people to one of our poetry forums, we declared:

"Outraged by so much loss and destruction in the name of unjust, deceitful and unjustified objectives—wars of conquest and domination in the name of protection against terrorism—the poets gathered here call for an immediate end to this spiral of violence and human degradation. We call for the end of the US and Israeli occupations, and for the beginning of a sincere process of reconciliation with justice and solidarity among the peoples. In times of tragedy and oppression, the voice of the poet shall be heard to celebrate hope."

"We knew well our voices were no match for the 150,000 US and British

troops occupying Iraq in a war that had already killed tens of thousands of Iraqis and hundreds of American and Allied troops. We knew that poetry, by itself, will never be enough to counter the machinery, structure and supra-structure of oppression and malfeasance in our existing human societies. But we also know that thought, concepts, words and feelings almost always precede or accompany human actions, if only at the unconscious level, and that includes wars, coups d'état and revolutions, as well. History will have proven our concerns right. In the meantime, the craving for peace and social justice, and the struggle to change life, continue.
—*Tontongi,* Boston, March 2007 (Edited by Jill Netchinsky)."[7]

***

It has been said that culture is often the first thing bureaucrats eliminate in budget cuts, but it can also be the only thing that remains viable when everything is swept away in chaos, in gangster-like governance, in daily fear and suffering, as it is unfortunately the case in Haiti today.

Indeed, when what Haiti represents historically is so soiled and challenged by the lamentable conditions that it faces today; while their homeland cries and is steeped in anguish, Haitian poets raise very high the banner of the "other" Haiti, exalting the beauty of its fauna and flora, revering the resistance of the ancestors while lighting the way for a better future.

In a new, trilingual anthology of Haitian poetry titled, *This Land, My Beloved.* Haitian poets bring to life other possibilities of being and living. It was released by Trilingual Press in October, 2023, featuring 47 authors plus a dozen translators. This anthology has already taken a place of predilection in Haitian trilingual literature, presenting an expression of beauty when the political landscape seems so ugly and painful.

The poets want their collective work to embody the resistance of a resilient people. In a sense, it constitutes an organ which conveys both a testimony of truth and a call to change. Through both poetry and praxis for change, the Haitian poets envision and work toward a future bright and hopeful, the extreme opposite of today's darkness.

The poets say that Haitian renewal must come from collective acts, requiring an applied praxis for a liberational redemption. Poets, throughout all cultures, lend an ideal of authenticity to the national project. For example, without the poetic inspiration of Boisrond Tonnerre, the secretary of Jean-Jacques Dessalines, the declaration of Haiti's independence might have been merely a flat formulation of interests.

Yes, poetry and poets still remain when everything else is swept away in the furrow of destruction, when our very dreams seem to vanish into nightmare, if not indifference. Poetry can be the anchor, and as we said in the Foreword of the anthology *This Land, My Beloved,* it can be also the only bright spot:

"In a world today where peoples are crushed under the joint assaults of the most dominating and aberrant militarism, as we see in Ukraine or in occupied Palestine, of the normalization of racism and hatred of the Other, as we see in the United States, or in the gangsterization of the State and of life itself, as people are currently experiencing in Haiti, it is rather astounding that our poets continue to produce, to sing the advent of another reality, to unveil the wealth of our island country Haiti on another order of valuation and determination of what is 'rich' and 'poor.' Indeed, how can a country that gives birth to such an outbreak of beauty and poetic wonders be called a 'poor' country?!" [8]

Can poetry stay silent in the face of evil? As of this writing in mid-December, 2024, one month before President-elect Donald Trump takes office, the liberal democracy which has governed the United States until now is seriously threatened by the neofascist Project 2025. The recent legislative gains by the extreme-right in Europe, just like the Trumpism in the US, testifies to a general trend where the rights and freedoms of the people are under tremendous attacks. Very fortunately, as we see in the recent England's election, in Mexico or in Syria, the wind of History is not always one-sided.

Victor Hugo could not remain silent in the face of Louis Napoléon Bonaparte's onslaught against the democratic project in France—many of his poems of the time, particularly the collection *Les Châtiments* ("The Punishments") are incendiary, political effusion of his conscience as a citizen, in the name of what is right and just. Writers in general, and poets in particular, feel often the irresistible urge to be the voice of the ultimate ethical imperative of their time.

—Tontongi, December, 2024

Notes

1. See my French profile of Massignon Coicou on the site Île en île, 2008: https://ile-en-ile.org/coicou/2024, *Guardian News & Media Limited* or its affiliates
2. Refaat Alareer, "If I Must Die", Revue *Tanbou*, edition Spring 2024. https://www.tanbou.com/2023/poetry.htm]
3. Benjamin Zephaniah, "Me? I thought, OBE me? Up yours, I thought", The Guardian, London, 2003. Zephaniah died from a brain tumor on December 7, 2023, at the age of 65.
4. For more on that incident and on García Lorca, see Ian Gibson's *Federico Garcia Lorca: A Life*, Pantheon Books, New York, 1989.
5. *Cry Out: Poets Protest the War*, published by George Braziller, Inc, 2003.
6. This portion of the text and some following paragraphs also appeared in the anthology *Poets Against the Killing Fields*, ed. Trilingual Press, Boston, 2003. "The series of poetry readings under the theme 'Poets Against the Killing Fields' took place in Cambridge and Boston,

Massachusetts, and also one in New York City. One particular reading atcthe Zeitgeist Gallery, on June 12, 2003, reunited the following poets, who read in rotation in a 'atelier' style: Aldo Tambellini, Askia Touré, Anna Wexler, Joselyn Almeida, Tontongi, Che Hicks, Red, Tanya Perez-Brennan, Neil Calender, Danielle Legros Georges, Margie Rasheed, Richard Wilhelm, Marc Goldfinger, Tony Van Der Meer. Jeff Freeman photographed and recorded the event, and C.C. Arshagra videotaped it. Brenda Walcott, Jill Netchinsky and L'Merche Frazier read in many of these events (one of them took place at the Artisans World Gallery, in Cambridge, MA)." [from Poets Against the Killing Fields.]

7. All the quoted passages, unless otherwise indicated, from Notes 6 to 9, are from Tontongi's Introduction to *Poets Against the Killing Fields*, ed. Trilingual Press, 2003.

8. This Land, My Beloved: A Trilingual Anthology of Contemporary Haitian Poetry, coedited by Elizabeth Brunazzi, Denizé Lauture, and Tontongi / Prefaced by Edwidge Danticat, Art & Editorial contribution by Jill Netchinsky, Charlot Lucien, and Michele Voltaire Marcelin. (ed. *Trilingual Press*, October 2023)

www.ingramcontent.com/pod-product-compliance
Lightning Source LLC
Chambersburg PA
CBHW060835190426
43197CB00040B/2626